For Barbara,
Becoz of the wonderful things she does.

CONTENTS

PREFACE

The Theory of Oz: Rediscovering the Aims of Education grew out of a commentary, "Off to See the Wizard," which I published in *Education Week* in 2002. I received at least half a dozen letters and e-mails of praise from readers after it appeared and a couple of requests to reprint it. The response was gratifying, but unrelated to my decision to expand the commentary into a book. I had decided to do that almost as soon as I began writing it. I can remember standing up from my desk on a rainy Saturday and going into the kitchen, where my wife was punching bread dough at the counter, and telling her, "You know, this could be a book." I explained that there seemed to be a lot more to say about Oz and education than the 1,500 words I was allowed. She didn't argue. She had lived and suffered with me through the writing of nine previous books. She just punched the dough a little harder.

Although I had no trouble finding material to fill a book, I did have some trouble finding a title for it. I considered calling the book *Lost in Oz* (too gloomy) and *The Wizard of Ed* (too reminiscent of the comic strip *Wizard of Id*) before finally settling on *The Theory of Oz*. Even then I wondered whether "theory" was the right term to describe what I was attempting. Somewhere I had gotten the idea that a full-blown theory of education must answer three questions: What educational aims should be cultivated? Why should they be cultivated? How should they be cultivated? I doubted my ability to come up with detailed answers to these questions or, if I did, to express them in the requisite jargon. Sure, I was a professor (of journalism!) and had been a school board president, but not everyone necessarily saw the latter as much of a qualification. As Mark Twain once observed, "God made the Idiot for practice and then He made the School Board."

I didn't feel secure in my choice of title until, late in my research, I read Seymour B. Sarason's *The Predictable Failure of Educational Reform* (1990)—not exactly an upbeat title itself. "Theory," Sarason wrote, "is a necessary myth that we construct to understand something we know we understand incompletely. Theory is a deliberate attempt to go beyond what we think are the erroneous explanations of others. It is intended to make a difference not only on the level of theory, but on the level of action, be it in a laboratory, a classroom, or a school." If that is indeed what theory is, then this book has an apt title, for it claims that today's schools have all kinds of shortcomings, that the solutions being proposed or implemented are inadequate, and that we should follow a different road, a road like the one Dorothy, Scarecrow, Tin Man, and Lion take to Oz.

Whatever I called the book, I wouldn't have been able to write it without help from family, friends, and colleagues. I want to thank my wife, Barbara, for sticking with me to the end when it might have been wiser, as the sign outside the Haunted Forest says, to turn back. I also want to thank our children, Gabe, Graham, Brittany, and Darla, for not kicking too much about appearing as characters in anecdotes scattered throughout the book. Lastly, I want to thank a few exceptional friends and colleagues—Joanne Loewenthal and Michael and Gina Dillon—for reading the book in manuscript form and commenting usefully on it. As Dorothy learns, good companions make some journeys not just enjoyable, but possible.

I

THE YELLOW BRICK SCHOOLHOUSE

What defines someone as educated? Is it getting a certain score on a standardized test? Is it passing through a prescribed curriculum? Is it being employable after high school? If you listen to politicians and educational bureaucrats, you might think so. But we need a better source of guidance than that.

Sometimes it seems as if everyone you meet has a half-cooked philosophy of education that he or she is only too eager to share with you. As cultural critic (and former public school teacher) Neil Postman observed, "There is no intellectual activity more American than quarreling about what education means."[1]

Of course, you don't have to be American to take part in the quarrel. From ancient times to the present, a bewildering array of philosophers and reformers have offered their own ideas about the aims of education:

Aristotle said the primary aim of education is "to produce a certain disposition in citizens, namely, to make them excellent and capable of performing noble actions."[2]

Immanuel Kant said education "aims at skill and perfection, not at informing the child on some matter, but at strengthening his mental powers."[3]

John Dewey said "education is the fundamental method of social
   progress and reform."[4]
Bertrand Russell said education "may be defined as the formation by
   means of instruction of certain mental habits and a certain outlook
   on life and the world."[5]
Alfred North Whitehead said "Education is the acquisition of the art
   of the utilisation of knowledge."[6]
Robert M. Hutchins said "There is a hierarchy of values. The task of
   education is to help us understand it, establish it, and live by it."[7]
Theodore Roszak said "Free human dialogue, wandering wherever
   the agility of the mind allows, lies at the heart of education."[8]
Jerome Bruner said "Education is a complex pursuit of fitting a culture to the needs of its members and of fitting its members and
   their ways of knowing to the needs of the culture."[9]

All this is enough, to paraphrase H. L. Mencken, to make even a post-
doc beg for mercy. It isn't just that when many so-called "experts" speak
or write about education, they almost invariably fall into impenetrable
jargon, or vaporous abstraction, or both. It is also that they often seem
to be recirculating the same old tired ideas. Perhaps that is what the jargon and abstraction are intended to hide.

In this book, I'm taking a new—and some might say daft—approach.
I plan to use one of the best-loved movies of all time, *The Wizard of Oz*,
as the scaffolding for an argument about the need to redefine the aims
of education. It is my premise that the four companions who skip arm in
arm down the Yellow Brick Road can each be seen as representing an
essential educational goal. When you add what Scarecrow wants (a
brain) to what Tin Man wants (a heart) to what Lion wants (courage) to
what Dorothy wants (home), you wind up with a fully educated person.
There is even a kind of graduation ceremony near the end of the movie,
during which the Wizard hands out awards and recognitions: a diploma
to Scarecrow, a heart-shaped watch to Tin Man, and a medal, the ironically named Triple Cross, to Lion.[10]

Mention *The Wizard of Oz* and most people immediately think of the
movie released by MGM in 1939, not the novel published by L. Frank
Baum in 1900. Baum wrote *The Wizard* partly in reaction to the classic
European fairy tale, which seemed to delight in terrifying children with

horrible incidents of blood-curdling cruelty. He wanted the book to be, in his words, "a modernized American fairy tale" that retained "the wonderment and joy" of Hans Christian Andersen and the Brothers Grimm but left out "the heart-aches and nightmares."[11]

Despite aspiring to modernity, Baum used the age-old pattern of the quest story, in which "a hero and his companions (usually all male) go in search of something virtually unobtainable yet infinitely desirable—the Water of Life, the Golden Bird, the dragon's treasure hoard—and at last, after a long and hazardous journey, find what they are seeking."[12] Baum's innovation lay in infusing this ancient story with a distinctly American flavor. The book doesn't begin in some kingdom long ago and far away, but in Kansas. Its protagonist is a little American girl, and the great and powerful Wizard is a con man from Omaha.

Baum also revised the traditional goal of the quest, playing on the irony that Dorothy and her companions already have within them the very things they seek. The movie version makes the point even more explicitly. Asked what she has learned on her bizarre journey through Oz, Dorothy (Judy Garland at her most wide-eyed) replies, "It's that if I ever go looking for my heart's desire again, I won't look any further than my own backyard; because if it isn't there, I never really lost it to begin with!"[13] Both book and movie suggest that we have enough brains and heart and courage—though we may not realize it just yet—to cope with anything that comes our way, from cyclones to wicked witches.

The Wizard of Oz ranks among the best-selling children's books of the twentieth century. Baum went on to write another 13 Oz books, including *The Land of Oz, Ozma of Oz, The Road to Oz,* and *The Patchwork Girl of Oz.* The books were so successful that when Baum died in 1919, his publishers wouldn't let the series die, too. They contracted with his widow to have another writer, Ruth Plumly Thompson, continue it. Thompson wrote one Oz book a year for the next 19 years.[14]

Juvenile readers may have loved *The Wizard of Oz,* but educators and critics didn't.[15] Until recently, standard reference works on children's literature either disparaged Baum's magnum opus or simply ignored it. In the 1969 edition of *A Critical History of Children's Literature,* Ruth Hall Viguers claimed that Baum wrote *The Wizard* in "such lifeless prose that rereading it in adulthood is a disappointment. Because there is no grace in the style, no subtlety in the storytelling to give conviction to the fantastic people and incidents, it lost nothing in translation to the screen."[16] Similarly, Humphrey Carpenter and Mari Prichard contended in *The Oxford Companion to Children's Literature* (1984) that "Baum's writing cannot be called distinguished. . . . The story is told considerably better in the 1939 MGM film version."[17]

That this was ever even a possibility would have come as a surprise to Baum's widow, Maud. While the movie was being made, co-producer Mervyn LeRoy asked her what she expected it to be like. "Oh, I suppose there'll be a Wizard in it," she said, "and a Scarecrow and a Tin Woodsman and maybe a Lion and a character named Dorothy. But that's all I expect, young man. You see, I've lived in Hollywood since 1910."[18]

Work on the movie neither started out auspiciously nor proceeded smoothly. W. C. Fields, for whom the part of the Wizard was written, turned it down. No director was assigned to the picture until shortly before shooting began, and then it had four different directors—Richard Thorpe for two weeks, George Cukor for three days, Victor Fleming for four months, and King Vidor for 10 days. Official credit for the screenplay went to Noel Langley, Florence Ryerson, and Edgar Allan Wallace, but another 10 writers tinkered with it. Aljean Harmetz, in *The Making of* The Wizard of Oz, her definitive history of Production #1060, concluded that the movie was more the product of the studio system than of any one individual.[19]

The movie took certain liberties with Baum's story. It added a lengthy Kansas prologue populated with new characters—Miss Gulch, Professor Marvel, the farmhands—who would later reappear in Oz in disguised form. It expanded and greatly darkened the role of the Witch, who was confined in the novel to a mere two chapters. It changed the book's silver shoes to ruby slippers (better for Technicolor). It made Oz a land that Dorothy dreams up after receiving a bump on her head, rather than an actual place, like Disney World or New Jersey. It gave extra emphasis to Dorothy's desire to return home, much to the dismay of the movie's lyricist, Yip Harburg, who complained: "The picture didn't need that 'Home, Sweet Home,' 'God Bless Our Home' tripe."[20]

Which makes it all the more remarkable, perhaps, that *The Wizard of Oz* became a classic. In 1989 it was one of 25 movies declared "national treasures" by the Library of Congress.[21] But as entertaining and imaginative as the movie is, full of indelible images and wonderful songs, the

key to its abiding popularity has been television. Starting in 1956, repeated televised showings of the movie transformed it into what
Harmetz, without hyperbole, called "an American institution."[22] It has
been seen by as many as 50 million viewers in a single showing and at
least a billion times altogether, more than any other movie in history.[23]

As a result, *The Wizard of Oz* has permeated popular culture. It provided the inspiration for the all-black musical *The Wiz*, the science fic-
tion movie *Zardoz*, and, as Suzanne Rahn wryly noted, "more than one
extravaganza on ice."[24] Allusions to it turn up in editorial cartoons,
comic strips, album covers, television shows, and advertisements. A
Subaru commercial some years ago had a hopelessly lost driver meet
Dorothy and Tin Man, while a recent Mastercard commercial has a hip,
twenty-something Dorothy so absorbed in online shopping that she
doesn't even notice the cyclone whirling her dog Toto around and
around. Certain lines from the movie have entered the language: "Toto,
I've a feeling we're not in Kansas anymore"; "Follow the Yellow Brick
Road"; "I'm melting!"

It was probably inevitable that *The Wizard of Oz*, like other cultural
myths, would attract the scrutiny of academics. They have subjected the
book and movie to a variety of interpretations. There might be some
value, or at least amusement, in summarizing a few:

- Henry M. Littlefield, in an article in *American Quarterly* in 1964,
  interpreted Baum's novel as a political allegory written amid the
  wreckage of the Populist movement of the 1890s. According to this
  interpretation, Baum saw that a potential alliance of farmers
  (Scarecrow) and urban industrial workers (Tin Man) had been subverted by the forces of finance and the shortcomings of Populist
  leaders, particularly William Jennings Bryan, the model for the
  Cowardly Lion. Dorothy's defeat of the wicked witches (the financial interests), befriending of Scarecrow, Tin Man, and Lion, and
  exposure of the Wizard (the federal government) as a powerless
  humbug was Baum's fairy-tale version of the political changes he
  desired.[25]
- Sheldon Kopp, in an article in *Psychology Today* in 1970, examined
  The Wizard of Oz as "a psychotherapeutic tale" in which Dorothy
  and her three companions resemble patients in crisis and the Wizard

their therapist.[26] Ten years later, David Magder, in the *Canadian Journal of Psychiatry*, similarly discussed *The Wizard of Oz* as "a parable about short-term psychotherapy."According to Magder, the Scarecrow, Tin Man, and Lion represent familiar syndromes: "low self-esteem based on the sense that one is not intelligent or capable of dealing with the world as one would like to, a sense of inability to respond emotionally or affectively, anxiety or fearfulness in dealing with the day to day problems of living."[27] After the therapist/Wizard intervenes, they are all more willing to perform difficult tasks voluntarily and with optimism.

- Todd S. Gilman, in an article he humorously titled "Aunt Em: Hate You! Hate Kansas! Taking the Dog. Dorothy," undertook with rather less humor "a reading of the film-text inspired by semiotics and Freudian psychoanalysis." Gilman argued that *The Wizard of Oz*, particularly in the character of Dorothy, reenacts "the tension between the conscious life of the ego, or self, and the repressed desires of the unconscious." Thus, the cyclone that smashes through Aunt Em and Uncle Henry's farm represents Dorothy's "buried rage, desire to punish those [adults] who have disappointed her, and need to escape."[28]

- David C. Downing, in an article in *Christianity and Literature* in 1982, called *The Wizard of Oz* "one of the most devastating exposes of institutional religion ever to reach the screen." Dorothy goes on a "pilgrimage" to seek the Wizard. She is joined on her "Grail-like quest" by Scarecrow, Tin Man, and Lion, "each in hopes of conquering some emptiness within." When they are admitted to the Wizard's palace, "its Gothic arches and other imposing architectural features" suggest a cathedral. The four, as Downing put it, "have come to a church-like structure to meet a god-like figure in order to have their problems resolved." The Wizard sends them on another quest, for the broomstick of the Wicked Witch. In the course of carrying it out, each of Dorothy's companions finds in himself the trait he thought he lacked. Later they discover something else: that the Wizard is a fraud. Yet, even though he is merely human, all have found what they sought by believing in him. "The implication here," Downing said, "is that the religious quest fulfills psychological needs regardless of its truth-value."[29]

Compared with the above, my own plan to approach *The Wizard of Oz* as a kind of educational fable seems pretty tame. But why attempt to redefine the aims of education at all? The answer to this is that school, as many students can tell you, sucks, and there isn't much prospect of it getting better anytime soon. In fact, the only real prospect is that it will get worse—more stultifying and pointless.

One recent survey found that most students in grades 10–12 don't believe their public schools are preparing them "very well" to know how to learn, get a good job, or go to college. Teacher confidence wasn't much higher. Fewer than one-fifth of the teachers surveyed gave the top rating to their schools. And in schools serving largely low-income families, teachers were even less likely to give their schools high ratings in preparing students for later life.[30]

Ironically, the future-oriented outlook of education may itself contribute to the problem. While schools strive to prepare students for the future, the students grow increasingly alienated and apathetic in the present. Dewey warned about the danger of this more than a century ago. Much of education fails, he wrote in "My Pedagogic Creed" (1897), because it "conceives the school as a place where certain information is to be given, where certain lessons are to be learned, or where certain habits are to be formed. The value of these is conceived as lying largely in the remote future; the child must do these things for the sake of something else he is to do; they are mere preparation. As a result they do not become a part of the life experience of the child and so are not truly educative."[31]

Just how little do students get from all the information given at school? A 2002 survey found that one in 10 Americans between ages 18 and 24 couldn't locate their own country on a map of the world. Only 17 percent could locate Afghanistan, though American-led forces had been waging war there, and only 13 percent could locate Iraq, though the United States was threatening to wage war there as well. Commenting on the findings, Robert A. Pastor, vice president of international affairs at American University, noted "the apparent retreat of young people from a global society in an era that doesn't allow such luxury." That may be overstating it. A full 34 percent knew that the Marquesas, the islands used for the *Survivor* show in 2001, were in the South Pacific. If we want young Americans to be better informed about geography, perhaps all we have to do is stage more television series in out-of-the-way places.[32]

One could go on forever quoting statistics that seem to prove school makes you stupid—for example, even though 70 percent of graduates enroll in college right after high school, more than 29 percent of them require remedial education.[33] Our public school system obviously suffers from all kinds of malaise. But, as in early medicine, the most popular cures often only aggravate the ailments.

The old misguided medical reliance on leeches and hot cups may have its closest academic equivalent in the current reliance on high-stakes testing. In January 2002, President George W. Bush signed into law the No Child Left Behind Act (NCLB), considered by many to be "perhaps the most significant change in federal regulation of public education in 30 years."[34] Its critics quickly redubbed it the "Leave No Child Untested Act."[35] The NCLB mandates that, beginning in 2005, all states annually test every third through eighth grader in reading and math and, beginning in 2007, in science, too. Schools that don't make "adequate yearly progress" in their students' test scores will be subject to a series of escalating penalties, culminating in loss of federal aid or the firing of their teachers and administrators.[36]

Although ostensibly designed to "raise standards" and hold schools "accountable," the NCLB has some little-noticed, oddball provisions buried in its 681 pages. These include requirements that districts certify their support of constitutionally protected prayer in school and that they provide military recruiters with the names, addresses, and telephone numbers of high school students.[37] The latter provision may not do much to improve student achievement—at least not as much as prayer, assuming, of course, that praying for the right answer actually works—but it will reduce recruiting costs, which have almost doubled from $6,500 to $11,600 per recruit in the past decade.[38]

Education has always had as one of its essential tasks fitting the individual to the particular grooves of his or her culture. Whether carried out in a classroom, forest, or sacred hut, unless education served this purpose, the culture would soon vanish. Its values would go unlearned, its traditions fall into disuse, its accumulated knowledge be forgotten. Self-preservation requires that the culture replicate itself in the minds and hearts of the young.

But, paradoxically, self-preservation also requires that the culture leave a space in which the individual can dream, question, experiment.

A culture that doesn't encourage the individual to occasionally go beyond the culture's norms, as well as provide through schooling the resources to do so, is doomed. It will become increasingly rigid. It will be unable to recognize changing circumstances or adapt to them. It will hunker down, stagnate, and pass into irrelevance.

"The aim of education," Elliot Eisner of Stanford University suggested, "is not to train an army that marches to the same drummer, at the same pace, toward the same destination. Such an aim may be appropriate for totalitarian societies, but it is incompatible with democratic ideals."[39] To truly thrive, a democracy like ours needs a public school system that values questions more than answers, discussion and debate more than certainty, risk-taking more than rules. Or, as Hutchins, writing in the early 1950s, said, "What belongs in education is what helps the student to learn to think for himself, to form an independent judgment, and to take his part as a responsible citizen."[40]

Half a century later, we are still waiting for what belongs in education to break through. But how can it when tests, tests, and more tests are squeezing everything else out? "Stuffing facts into your head doesn't help you think better," Alfie Kohn, a leading critic of the testing craze, noted. According to Kohn, "the time spent stuffing is time *not* spent analyzing or inventing or communicating, making distinctions or drawing connections."[41] Rather than raising standards, high-stakes testing—and the desperate atmosphere that accompanies it—may have the ironic effect of depressing them.

In theory, school is supposed to instill "high levels of literacy and logic and the capacity to think critically."[42] In practice, school often does the exact opposite. It conditions students to put up with mind-numbing boredom. It teaches them to obey instructions. It equips them to become the kind of people who take cues for how to live from movies and television, who seek happiness at the mall, who believe the star-spangled lies that politicians tell them.

Ask yourself, would a society that valued students as future citizens, rather than as current or potential consumers, educate them quite the way ours does? Would it have them watch the movie *Shakespeare in Love* in 11th-grade English, but not actually read Shakespeare?[43] Would it subject them to rounds and rounds of standardized tests and use the results to sort them into invidious categories—roughly, those who will grow up to shop at Wal-Mart (or, worse, work there) and those who will grow up to shop at more upscale stores? Would it allow corporations to build nests in their heads?

Since 1990, commercial activities in schools have risen 473 percent.[44] The activities range from product sales (exclusive contracts for soft drinks) to direct advertising (the display of a corporate logo on vending machines) to market research on students (taste testing, online profiling).[45] What schools get in exchange for this is money, teaching materials, technology resources, and sports equipment. What businesses get is a captive audience.[46]

Schools have become, in effect, pimps for the chamber of commerce. Our public school system may not teach students to read for pleasure, write well, think critically, or be responsible citizens, but it does prepare them to accept advertising as natural and good and to see consumption as a sure path to personal fulfillment, especially when traveled in the kind of giant SUVs favored by inner-city drug dealers and third-world death squads.

What else does the system prepare them for? To step on each other in the pursuit of honors. To treat the different with contempt and the weak without mercy. To suspect intellect. To lie and cheat and plagiarize so long as they don't get caught. To sleepwalk through the day.

Students recognize the shortcomings of school to a degree that adults generally don't. The National Commission on the High School Senior Year was taken aback by what interviews with students revealed about the "class structure" of school. The structure worked for some students, the ones who were able to demonstrate prowess in academics, sports, or music, but worked against many others. In the commission's words, "Everyone else faded into a blur, with no teacher, counselor, or other adult knowing him or her well."[47] Mandatory testing, though touted as a cure-all, isn't likely to help these forgotten students, often poor and of color, to feel valued or connected. To the contrary, more layers of testing will probably just add to their feelings of worthlessness and inadequacy.

I intend to follow the Yellow Brick Road to something better, and you are invited. On the way, we will meet Dorothy and her three strange-looking companions. We will discuss the objects of their quest and why perhaps they should be the objects of ours, too. But how far, I wonder, must we go before we finally arrive at brains and heart and courage and know the place as home?

NOTES

1. Neil Postman, *The End of Education: Redefining the Value of School* (New York: Knopf, 1996), 139.

2. Quoted in William K. Frankena, *Three Historical Philosophies of Education: Aristotle, Kant, Dewey* (Chicago: Scott Foresman, 1965), 7.

3. Quoted in Frankena, *Three Historical Philosophies*, 87.

4. John Dewey, "My Pedagogic Creed," in *Dewey on Education*, ed. Martin S. Dworkin (New York: Teachers College Press, 1959), 29.

5. Quoted in Frankena, *Three Historical Philosophies*, 6.

6. A. N. Whitehead, *The Aims of Education and Other Essays* (New York: Macmillan, 1929), 7.

7. Robert M. Hutchins, *The Conflict in Education in a Democratic Society* (New York: Harper and Brothers, 1953), 72.

8. Quoted in Postman, *The End of Education*, 27.

9. Jerome Bruner, *The Culture of Education* (Cambridge, Mass.: Harvard University Press, 1996), 43.

10. I explored this idea in a shorthand form in "Off to See the Wizard," *Education Week*, December 11, 2002, 29, 31.

11. L. Frank Baum, *The Wizard of Oz* (New York: Tor, 1993), xx.

12. Suzanne Rahn, *The Wizard of Oz: Shaping an Imaginary World* (New York: Twayne, 1998), 9. See also Bernard Welt, "St. Dorothy of Oz," in *Mythomania* (Los Angeles: Art Issue Press, 1996), 41–45.

13. Noel Langley, Florence Ryerson, and Edgar Allan Woolf, *The Wizard of Oz: The Screenplay*, ed. Michael Patrick Hearn (New York: Delta, 1989), 128.

14. Aljean Harmetz, *The Making of* The Wizard of Oz (New York: Limelight, 1977), 311, 314–16.

15. See Russel B. Nye, "An Appreciation," in *The Wizard of Oz and Who He Was*, ed. Martin Gardner and Russel B. Nye, rev. ed. (East Lansing: Michigan State University Press, 1994), 1–17.

16. Quoted in Rahn, *Wizard*, 17.

17. Quoted in Rahn, *Wizard*, 18.

18. Rahn, *Wizard*, 111.

19. Harmetz, *Making*, 20; Rahn, *Wizard*, 110; Harold Meyerson and Ernie Harburg, *Who Put the Rainbow in* The Wizard of Oz? *Yip Harburg, Lyricist* (Ann Arbor: University of Michigan, 1993), 120.

20. Quoted in Meyerson and Harburg, *Rainbow*, 153.

21. Rahn, *Wizard*, 109.

22. Harmetz, *Making*, 291.

23. Rahn, *Wizard*, 9.

24. Rahn, *Wizard*, 11.

25. Henry M. Littlefield, "The Wizard of Oz: Parable on Populism," *American Quarterly* 16 (Spring 1964): 47–58.

26. Sheldon Kopp, "The Wizard of Oz Behind the Couch," *Psychology Today*, March 1970, 70.

27. David Magder, "The Wizard of Oz: A Parable of Brief Psychotherapy," *Canadian Journal of Psychiatry* 25 (1980): 564–65.

28. Todd S. Gilman, "'Aunt Em: Hate You! Hate Kansas! Taking Dog. Dorothy': Conscious and Unconscious Desire in *The Wizard of Oz*," *Children's Literature Association Quarterly* 20 (Winter 1995): 162–63. Along the same lines, Salman Rushdie contended that the movie's "driving force is the inadequacy of adults, and how the weakness of grown-ups forces children to take control of their own destinies and so, ironically, grow up themselves." Rushdie, *The Wizard of Oz* (London: British Film Institute, 1992), 10.

29. David C. Downing, "Waiting for Godoz: A Post-Nasal Deconstruction of *The Wizard of Oz*," *Christianity and Literature* 31 (Winter 1982): 28–30.

30. Erik W. Robelen, "Survey: Students Give Schools Middling Marks," *Education Week*, October 16, 2002, 10.

31. Dewey, "Pedagogic Creed," 23–24.

32. "Young Americans Get 'D' on Geography Survey," *Poughkeepsie Journal*, November 21, 2002, 4A. The survey results are also available at www.nationalgeographic.com/geosurvey.

33. Debra Viadero, "U.S. Urged to Rethink High School," *Education Week*, January 24, 2001, 1, 12.

34. *The New Accountability: An Implementation Guide to the No Child Left Behind Act* (Albany: New York State School Boards Association, 2002), 1.

35. Michelle J. Lee, "Schools Grapple with Federal Law," *Poughkeepsie Journal*, December 17, 2002, 1A.

36. *Accountability*, 1.

37. *Accountability*, 4.

38. Michelle J. Lee, "Act Gives Students' Names to Military Recruiters," *Poughkeepsie Journal*, December 17, 2002, 5A.

39. Alfie Kohn, *The Schools Our Children Deserve* (Boston: Houghton Mifflin, 1999), 94.

40. Hutchins, *Conflict*, 13.

41. Kohn, *Schools*, 54.

42. National Commission on the High School Senior Year, "The Lost Opportunity of Senior Year: Finding a Better Way," Summary of Findings, January 2001, 3.

43. The experience of my 16-year-old daughter at a rural high school.

44. Kirstin Larsen, "Commercialism in Schools," *Updating School Board Policies* 33 (October–November 2002): 1.

45. Larsen, "Commercialism," 1.

46. Only 19 states have adopted laws regulating commercialism in schools, and some laws permit, rather than prohibit, specific commercial activities. Larsen, "Commercialism," 2.

47. National Commission on the High School Senior Year, "Lost Opportunity," 4.

2

BRAINS

It is depressing how often school reformers cite the need for a hard-charging, butt-kicking American workforce as the primary reason we should adopt their proposed reforms. One reformer might be arguing for smaller class sizes and another for a broader curriculum, but both will claim that their ideas, if implemented, will contribute in the long run to making American workers more fearsome and efficient in the global competition for markets.

In an essay titled "Preparing Students for the World," Jaime Escalante, the celebrated math teacher portrayed in the movie *Stand and Deliver*, urged other teachers to emulate his tough, take-no-prisoners teaching style as a means to strengthen the economy. "The skills and expertise of a nation's workforce are the foundation of the nation's economic success," he explained. "Right now in this country that foundation is weak. High schools are not producing students to stand and deliver in the face of the twenty-first century."[1] Curiously, consultants Richard L. Curwin and Allen N. Mendler offered almost the exact same justification for their touchy-feely approach to violence prevention. The "problem of violence," they said, is undermining the "instructional initiative needed to transform schools into the technologically sophisticated institutions demanded by today's workplace."[2] Whether teacher- or learner-centered, authoritarian or progressive, most reformers seem unable to conceive of school as anything but boot camp for the corporate armies of the future.

The irony is that the work world for which schools should supposedly be preparing students doesn't exist. School reformers mislead when they present postmodern economic life in terms of the United States versus everyone else. After all, even American automakers, once the pivot of the nation's prosperity, aren't exclusively American anymore. And why should students care anyway about becoming exemplary employees? The corporations that now dominate the economy don't care especially about being exemplary employers. You can be hard working and well trained, but as recent headlines suggest, you can still wake up one morning to find your corporate employer has suspended your benefits, plundered your pension, or outsourced your job.

Not that this has prevented the concept of school as a kind of job fair from trickling down to the grassroots level. At the end of the 2003 school year, the principal of the middle school that my youngest daughter, Darla, attends sent out letters encouraging parents to have their child read at least an hour a day in the summer. The district had experimented the previous few summers with a list of required reading, but some parents and school board members had furiously objected to it as an unwarranted intrusion on vacation time. Now, to justify his controversial recommendation that kids pick up a book or two during July and August, the principal pointed to the need for the nation's workforce to maintain its competitive edge. "As America has entered the twenty-first century," he wrote, "the economy has shifted . . . from industrial to technological. With this shift has come the need for increased mental skills in the American workforce. Thus children are being asked to spend more time-on-task to develop these higher-order thinking and processing skills"—in other words, to read. Who knew that the fate of the economy might hinge on whether Darla and her 13-year-old classmates crack open the latest hefty volume in the Harry Potter series.

Like the principal, Scarecrow in *The Wizard of Oz* recognizes the job value of being mentally sharp. When he first meets Dorothy, Scarecrow complains about the crows that come from miles around to eat in his field and laugh in his face. "Oh," he moans, "I'm a *failure* because I haven't got a brain."[3] But as useful as a brain would be in helping him do his job, that isn't the only reason he wants one. He remarks—significantly, via song—that if he had a brain, he "could while away the hours / Conferrin' with the flowers / Consultin' with the rain."[4] The prospect is so inviting that ordinary speech can't possibly express his eagerness and joy. Only singing can.

Scarecrow is essentially echoing what Aristotle once said: "Learning something is the greatest of pleasures not only to the philosopher, but also to the rest of mankind, however small their capacity for it."[5] Educators seem to have largely forgotten this, as an incident that occurred back when I was president of a school board underlines.

Elementary school administrators and teachers were presenting to the board a grade-by-grade review of desired student outcomes. The reading goals for second graders, explained with overheads and handouts by one of the school's two deans, were identified as mastery in word analysis, vocabulary, and comprehension. The dean went into some detail about each of the goals. Students would show mastery in vocabulary, for example, by "expanding sight word vocabulary through appropriate words lists"; "increasing the use of multiple meanings"; and "expanding word meanings through the use of synonyms, homonyms, and antonyms."[6]

It was a long meeting, made longer still by the fact that, as thorough and well rehearsed as the presentation was, it contained not one reference to promoting a love of reading, or of any other subject, among students. "I would dance and be merry," Scarecrow sings, "Life would be a ding-a-derry / If I only had a brain."[7] None of the presenters saw this kind of intellectual enjoyment as a necessary goal of school. Instead, they were focused on teaching technical skills, such as "identifying and producing consonant blend and digraph sounds" or "identifying grade-level appropriate word families."[8] Although these things are clearly important, they aren't ends in themselves. They are often just taught as if they were.

Small wonder, then, that there has been resistance in the district to summer reading. Why wouldn't there be when students are taught to read not so they can enjoy stories or the play of ideas, but so they can be tested? We can shake our heads and cluck disapprovingly about how kids don't read today, but you wouldn't want to read either if you were accustomed to experiencing reading as a chore, not a pleasure.

"To destroy the Western tradition of independent thought," Robert M. Hutchins said, "it is not necessary to burn the books. All we have to do is leave them unread for a couple of generations."[9] Adults tend to blame movies, television, video games, the Internet, and hip hop, the whole frenetic landscape of popular culture, for distracting young people from the older, slower, deeper rewards of reading. But schools have had a part in this, too, by neglecting the value of reading for its own sake, as an enviable activity of an enlightened mind.

Scarecrow already has a pretty good mind; he just doesn't realize it. Nonetheless, Scarecrow understands better than many educators do the latent power and glory of brains. "Oh, I could tell you why," he sings in happy anticipation of getting some, "The ocean's near the shore, / I could think of things I never thunk before / And then I'd sit and think some more."[10] Scarecrow's attitude seems to be that thinking is a worthwhile activity in and of itself, that it doesn't need an economic rationale to justify it, that using your brains to appreciate the wonder and mystery of existence is justification enough. Being brainless, in other words, isn't a matter of how few brains you have. It is a matter of how you use the brains you've got. Perhaps the degree to which you use them with joy and reverent awe is precisely the degree to which you are well educated.

BRAIN FREEZE

My students, most of whom are college juniors and seniors majoring in journalism or public relations, are capable of some truly atrocious writing. I'm not referring to stories that contain a few misplaced modifiers and a couple of disagreements in number. I'm referring to writing that is flat-out inept, the apparent product of space aliens or aphasics. Instead of writing "laundry chute," a student will write "laundry shoot." Instead of writing "witchcraft," a student will write "which craft." Instead of writing "futile effort," a student will write "feudal effort." When I shared the last with a colleague, poet and English professor Dennis Doherty, he joked that maybe the subject of the sentence was digging a moat. These aren't the worst examples I can cite either. Just last semester one of my students wrote "The room smelled like incest" when she meant to write—at least I hope she meant to write—"incense."

My first reaction to this kind of primeval prose is to groan out loud. My second is to shake my head in disbelief that students who claim to want to be professional writers read so little that they can't distinguish between similar-sounding words (one of them, for example, attributed a child's death to a "genital," instead of "congenital," heart condition). My third reaction is to wonder what the hell is happening in high schools and lower grades.

Not too much, it turns out. The National Commission on Writing in America's Schools and Colleges recently reported that two-thirds of high school seniors write English papers less than once a month and that three-quarters have never received a writing assignment in history or social studies. The commission further found that fourth graders spend about 85 percent more time each week watching television than they do writing. It dubbed writing the "Neglected 'R.'"[11]

The commission was convened by the College Board, the company that creates and administers the Scholastic Aptitude Test (SAT), which functions as a college entrance exam. The commission's report comes at a time when the College Board is preparing to include a writing requirement in the SAT.[12] Here, as seemingly everywhere in education today, concern over student learning loops back to plans for a new and tougher regimen of student testing.

That schools have plenty of room for improvement is beyond dispute. There is the rocking testimony of "The Boss," Bruce Springsteen, who attended Freehold (N.J.) Regional High School. "We busted out of class," he sings in his sandpapery voice, "had to get away / from those fools / We learned more from a three-minute / record, baby, than we ever learned in / school."[13] And there is the scientific testimony of statistics. Nearly one in five high school seniors can't identify the main idea in what they have read. Nearly two in five seniors haven't mastered the use of fractions, percentages, and averages. Nearly a third of high school graduates who go on to college require remedial courses.[14]

The statistics pertaining to minority students are especially grim. The National Task Force on Minority Achievement, another blue-ribbon panel convened by the College Board, reported in 1999 that only 17 percent of black and 24 percent of Latino high school seniors were proficient in reading, and that only 4 percent of blacks were proficient in math and science. At Berkeley (Calif.) High School, considered one of the top public high schools in the country, 90 percent of the black male students receive a D or F on every single report card. Most of the school's white students "graduate and go off to four-year colleges," while most of its black and Latino students "drop out, flunk out, or go off to junior college, low-wage jobs, or jail."[15]

The issue of student achievement is real. It is the proposed solution—standardized testing of more students, at more grade levels, in more subjects—that is illusory. When President George W. Bush signed into law the No Child Left Behind Act (NCLB), he predicted "great progress" once its testing provisions took effect in 2005.[16] This outcome is about as likely as the Wicked Witch of the West winning a beauty pageant. States can annually test third through eighth graders, as the NCLB requires, and still never address the factors that condemn some students to almost certain failure and send others on to success.

Chief among these factors is economic circumstances. In a long, heavily footnoted report to the New York State Board of Regents in 2003, the State Aid Work Group called the relationship between poverty and student achievement "pervasive." "As student poverty in a district increases," the report said, "academic performance declines." It added that New York City, Rochester, Buffalo, Syracuse, and Yonkers have the highest poverty and among the worst achievement in the state. Three out of four students in the New York City School District, for example, are at risk of not graduating from high school.[17]

The report also noted that "a distinct relationship exists between spending, student risk, and academic performance." Simply put, the more a school district spends per student, the greater the student achievement.[18]

High-stakes testing of the sort envisioned by the NCLB won't wipe out student poverty or increase per-student spending. It won't improve students' home life or raise the level of their parents' education. It won't silence "the rumor of inferiority" that continues to plague black students or change the fact that school districts with the largest percentage of minority students have the largest percentage of teachers without certification.[19] And yet these are the very things—family background, economic status, racial and ethnic prejudice, teacher quality—that end up determining how well kids do in school.

The increasing emphasis on testing may not merely be unproductive; it may actually be counterproductive. Two recent studies, both conducted by the Educational Policy Studies Laboratory at Arizona State University, suggest nothing less. One study examined data from 28 states that already give high-stakes tests—tests that students must pass to be promoted to the next grade or to receive a high school diploma. Researchers compared results on the state tests with the performance of students on other widely recognized assessments, including the SAT, the American College Test (ACT), and Advanced Placement (AP) exams. They found that students in states with high-stakes testing programs performed no better on the SAT, ACT, and AP exams than students in the rest of the country. In fact, after implementing high-stakes testing, twice as many states slipped against the national average as improved.

"Teachers are focusing so intently on the high-stakes tests that they are neglecting other things that are ultimately more important," said Audrey L. Amrein, who wrote the study with David C. Berliner. "In theory, high-stakes tests should work because they advance the notions of high standards and accountability. But students are being trained so narrowly . . . they are having a hard time branching out and understanding general problem solving."[20]

The other study by the Educational Policy Studies Laboratory found higher numbers of dropouts and lower graduation rates in 16 states where students must pass an exit exam to graduate. It also found:

- Higher numbers of low-performing students being suspended or expelled before testing days or being reclassified as special education or of limited English language proficiency so they will be exempt from testing.
- Reduced offerings in art, music, science, social studies, and physical education because these subjects are less often tested.
- Higher numbers of teachers, particularly in urban areas, "teaching to the test"—limiting instruction to only those things sure to be tested and drilling students on test-taking strategies.
- Instances of cheating by teachers and other school employees under pressure to raise test scores.[21]

There is worse news. The new state tests are norm-referenced, meaning scores on them don't measure competence in a subject area. Unlike criterion-referenced tests, which tell us how well students know or do something by comparing their scores to a given standard, norm-referenced tests only tell how well students compare to each other. "By design," Deborah Meier pointed out, "50 percent of the students' scores will fall below the median—and 50 percent above. This would be true no matter what the competence of the population actually is."[22] To use norm-referenced tests to evaluate how well teachers have taught or students have learned is, in the words of another school reformer, "like measuring temperature with a tablespoon."[23] But states use them in just that way.

Why? Perhaps because the supporters of testing dislike teachers and want to see them squirm. When I was on the school board, I repeatedly heard complaints not only about individual teachers, but also about teachers as a group. They get too much time off, people would say with a hint of envy. They have too much job security. They make too much money.

Although some people have teachers in their sights, students are the ones most often hit. I read somewhere about a school district that on testing days must put extra janitors on duty to clean up the vomit from all the students overcome by test anxiety. In my own school district, teachers have shortened recess in some grades and eliminated it in others so they can spend more time preparing students for the state tests. My district also has begun giving standardized tests to second graders, a grade level lower than required by the NCLB, in hopes of identifying students who need remedial help. No one seems to care that students that young may not yet have the physical coordination to properly fill in the bubbles on their answer sheets.

One of the most persistent and impassioned opponents of high-stakes testing, Susan Ohanian, believes that its backers are trying to impose on the country a political agenda camouflaged as academic excellence. "This is the agenda of class war," she wrote, "that devours the young of the poor as well as the middle- and upper-class young who don't respond well to lock-step commands, i.e., kids who don't want to go to MIT and become technocrats."[24] Actually, even the kids who do want to go to MIT get eaten up by the system.

Denise Clark Pope followed five high-achieving high school students for her book *Doing School.* She found that instead of thinking deeply about course content, the students "focus on managing the workload and honing strategies that will help them achieve." These strategies sometimes include "kissing up, lying, and cheating." Pope saw the students as victims of what she called the "grade trap," the fear that lower grades and test scores might jeopardize future wealth and well-being.[25]

The students recognized the bind they were in—and resented it. "I am just a machine with no life at this place," one complained to Pope. "This school turns students into robots. I have been thinking about it a lot; I am a robot just going page by page, doing work, doing the routine." The students longed for more moments of intellectual engagement, more opportunities to study subjects that interested them, as opposed to "drudgingly pursuing high marks without necessarily learning the material."[26]

We have developed a system that, with its emphasis on tests and grades, practically demands bad teaching, boring curriculum, and brain-dead students. Noted educators from Jean Piaget to John Dewey to Jerome Bruner to Alfie Kohn have long warned against the kind of schooling that the NCLB is calling forth. Piaget: "Little learning is retained when it is learned on command."[27] Dewey: "There is no obvious social motive for the acquirement of mere learning, there is no clear social gain thereat."[28] Bruner: "Telling children and then testing them on what they have been told inevitably has the effect of producing bench-bound learners whose motivations for learning are likely to be extrinsic to the task—pleasing the teacher, getting into college, artificially maintaining self-esteem."[29] Kohn: "Drilling isn't teaching."[30]

If those in charge of our schools haven't listened to these experts, perhaps they will listen to the Wizard of Oz, who, after all, is even more famous. The Wizard shows a certain sly disdain for academic achievements when he confers an honorary Th.D.—Doctor of Thinkology—on Scarecrow near the end of the movie. "Why, anybody can have a brain," the Wizard says. "That's a very mediocre commodity. . . . Back where I come from, we have universities, seats of great learning—where men go to become great thinkers, and when they come out, they think deep thoughts—with no more brains than you have—*but!* they have one thing you haven't got! A diploma." The Wizard presents a parchment scroll with seal and ribbon to Scarecrow, who then puts a finger to his head and spouts the Pythagorean theorem: "The sum of the square roots of any two sides of an isosceles triangle is equal to the square root of the remaining side."[31]

Scarecrow seems as surprised as anyone by what pops out of his mouth. Although proud of his newfound knowledge, he is curiously disengaged from it, like a student who learns something for a test and immediately forgets it once the test is over. Did Scarecrow come so far and risk so much just for this? Aren't brains meant to be used for more?

BRAINSTORM

By the end of *The Wizard of Oz*, Scarecrow may sound like a high school senior cramming for an exit exam, but for most of the movie, he puts his brains to other—and, I would argue, better—use. All the while, ironically, he believes he doesn't have any brains. Like today's educational policymakers, he equates having brains with meeting a rigid set of academic requirements, such as sitting through certain classes or scoring high on certain tests.

It quickly becomes apparent, though, that Scarecrow is no dummy, despite being stuffed with straw. When Dorothy first meets him on the Yellow Brick Road, she asks, "How can you talk if you haven't got a brain?" To which he replies: "I don't know. But some people without brains do an awful lot of talking, don't they?"[32] Dorothy is impressed by this folksy wisdom, and so should be viewers.

As Dorothy and Scarecrow (later joined by Tin Man and Lion) continue on their journey, they face various obstacles and dangers that Scarecrow uses his brains to overcome. It is Scarecrow who, when he and Dorothy are hungry, has the idea of taunting some ill-tempered apple trees into pelting them with apples. It is also Scarecrow who, when the doorman at the Wizard's palace demands proof that Glinda sent them, thinks to point to the ruby slippers on Dorothy's feet. It is Scarecrow again who, when Dorothy is captured by the Wicked Witch, hatches a plan to rescue her. And, finally, it is Scarecrow who, when he and the others are being held at spearpoint in the Witch's castle, suddenly jerks Tin Man's arm so his ax comes down and cuts a rope fixed to the wall, causing a huge circular chandelier with flaming candles to fall on the Winkie guards.[33]

What motivates Scarecrow to use his brains is only rarely what motivates students today to use theirs. Whether Scarecrow is outwitting apple trees or devising a rescue plan, he is using his brains for pro-social ends—to protect and promote the welfare of the group. Most schools promote quite the opposite. In class, Alfie Kohn pointed out, "children are forced to work either against one another [by competing for grades, honors, etc.] or apart from one another [by learning individually at separate desks]. The chance to work *with* one another, to learn social skills and caring, is left to happen by itself during recess, at lunch, or after school. This single fact goes a long way toward explaining why people in our society tend to regard others as potential obstacles to their own success."[34]

Even I, who have spent pages criticizing a system that dehumanizes students, that turns them into competitors, am caught in its pull. My second oldest child, Graham, didn't become valedictorian of his high school class by growing up in a home where grades were treated as a mere byproduct of learning, and he didn't go on to an Ivy League university purely by chance. Now that my third oldest, Brittany, is applying to college, I again find myself doing things I don't necessarily admire.

Britt needs another 20 points on her SAT to qualify for a half-tuition scholarship at the college she most wants to attend. My wife and I are trying to squeeze them out of her by sending her to a private tutoring center called the Finish Line. The name sums up just about everything that is wrong with school: the vicious competition, the success ethos, the survival of the fewest. I know all this, and still I keep entering my kids in the race. Scarecrow, who longs for external validation, the reward of shiny academic trinkets, despite being plenty smart without it, would understand.

BRAIN TEASER

After a year of observing life at a California high school, journalist Meredith Maran concluded, "If the purpose of educating our children is to prepare a tiny number of them to own and run the country, a slightly larger number of them to ensure the profitability of our corporations, and the vast majority of them to flip burgers, clean our hotel rooms, and fill our prisons—in short, to maintain our greed-driven, stratified society as it now exists—then we are doing an excellent job, and we should change nothing."[35] But, of course, we expect more from our schools and for our children than that.

Or at least we say we do. We say we want every child to reach his or her potential. We say no child should be left behind. What exactly would it take for us to live up to our rhetoric? Ellen J. Langer, a Harvard psychologist, believes that it would take the spread of mindful learning.[36]

A mindful approach to learning is marked by "the continuous creation of new categories; openness to new information; and an implicit awareness of more than one perspective." In contrast, teachers today tend to follow a "paint-by-numbers approach" that inhibits creativity and undermines thought. Several powerful assumptions, or "myths," govern most teaching, including that "Rote memorization is necessary in education" and that "There are right and wrong answers." These myths virtually ensure a kind of mindlessness—that instead of students learning to think for themselves, they will learn to think only what their teachers have approved.[37]

Like Langer, Deborah Meier, who founded progressive schools in both New York City and Boston, claims that students will benefit more from new habits of mind than from higher standards or test-driven curriculum. She suggests that students be taught to regularly ask questions about:

1. Evidence (How do we know what we know?)
2. Point of view (Whose perspective does this represent?)
3. Connections (How is this related to that?)
4. Supposition (How might things have been otherwise?)
5. Relevance (Why is this important?)[38]

Scarecrow would seem to embody many of the qualities of mind that Langer and Meier consider essential. Never having been taught in school that there are such things as right and wrong answers, he is open to new ideas. He can improvise solutions to situations that would probably leave the rest of us, burdened by mindlessly memorized old information, scratching our heads.

But even Scarecrow's ingenuity has its limits. He falls for the Wizard's charade no less than Dorothy, Tin Man, and Lion do, trembling just like them before the throne of the great and powerful Oz. For all his brains, Scarecrow reveals a strange willingness to suspend disbelief, to accept orders at face value, to defer to authority. Toto, not Scarecrow, pulls the curtain aside and exposes the Wizard as a fraud. Scarecrow is too intimidated by the Wizard's gaudy display of power—the lofty hall decorated in green and silver glass, the gigantic, shadowy head hovering above the throne, the booming and echoing voice—to be able to see him for what he actually is.

There may be no higher purpose for American public schools than to create a public that regards official power without awe, that asks questions, takes risks, and values the clash and clamor of debate. Schools now do a very poor job of creating such a public. By the time students reach me, in their third or fourth year of college, the vast majority are already bored by politics and disillusioned with public life. They don't keep up on the issues, vote in elections, or otherwise behave as responsible citizens. The idea that they should almost amuses them.

For democracy to work, students must leave school imbued with the democratic spirit. One thing for sure, if that ever happens, it won't be because more states are making more students suffer through more tests. If we want students to become active citizens, then we need to give them some actual experience in citizenship at school. "Students should not play life, or study it merely, while the community supports them at this expensive game," Thoreau said, "but earnestly live it from beginning to end. How could youths better learn to live than by at once trying the experiment of living."[39] Proper education for democracy requires that we reconceive school as a kind of laboratory of community life, where students are free to muck around with the specimens and make mistakes as well as discoveries.

What I'm suggesting goes beyond students serving on the prom committee or student council. It even goes beyond students serving as quasi-members of school boards, as allowed under legislation recently signed into law in New York State.[40] What I'm suggesting is more or less what Jerome Bruner once suggested, that students be given greater responsibility for setting and achieving goals in all aspects of school.[41] Students should help maintain school buildings and grounds—painting, planting, picking up litter. They should contribute to decisions about which classes and extracurricular activities the school offers. They should take part in formulating and perhaps even enforcing the school's disciplinary code. Only then will students know, as citizens of a democracy must, that rights come with certain responsibilities and that private interests can't always trump the public interest.

Anyone familiar with school administrators or school board members can probably already hear them objecting to this. Not that they disapprove of educating young people to be good citizens. It is just that their idea of good citizenship often resembles something out of the Third Reich. Given a choice, many would prefer that students be dull and obedient rather than free-thinking and obstreperous. I can remember a high school principal proudly telling me about how he had the benches removed from the school courtyard so students would have one less place to linger. He regarded the student body as dangerous, a volatile mixture of hormones and hair gel in need of constant supervision and control. The worst part is, after retiring as principal a few years ago, this man became an adjunct professor at a graduate school of education and has since taught his sad administrative philosophy to others.

The Wizard of Oz teaches a more valuable lesson. Near the end of the movie, as the Wizard prepares to depart with Dorothy for Kansas in a hot-air balloon, he informs the people of Oz that until he returns, Scarecrow, "by virtue of his highly superior brains, shall rule in my stead," assisted by Tin Man, "by virtue of his magnificent heart," and Lion, "by virtue of his courage."[42] This implies that brains, heart, and courage are the key civic virtues and the only sure basis for the well-run polity. It also implies that brains aren't sufficient by themselves, but must be supplemented and supported by heart and courage. Brains without courage may result in mere wishful thinking, while brains without heart may result in cruelty, the inquisitions and purges that have historically accompanied zealous attempts at social engineering. Brains, heart, and courage work best in combination with each other. We can't slight any one of them in educating the young without creating the potential for havoc.

BRAIN DEATH

All of us have seen movies that warn against overreliance on computers and other types of machines. Two that have stayed with me are *2001: A Space Odyssey*, in which the computer HAL starts feeling uppity and tries to murder the crew of a space station, and *The Forbin Project*, in which a U.S. military computer named Colossus and its Soviet counterpart join forces to enslave the human race. *The Wizard of Oz* can also be interpreted as a cautionary tale about the dangers of technology. What is the contraption that the Wizard uses to produce a huge, terrifying image of himself on a throne but a kind of proto-laptop?

The image that the Wizard projects is completely misleading. "You humbug!" Scarecrow exclaims when he finally meets the little old Wizard in the roly-poly flesh. We might say much the same thing about the belief that technology will provide the cure for whatever ails education—humbug!

Most educators say nothing of the kind, though. They persist in expecting miraculous breakthroughs from the application of the latest technology to schooling. At a conference of the New York State Association of Small City School Districts in 2003, school officials brainstormed ways to "make learning more appealing to the Internet generation." They discussed the possibility of using "Hollywood animation to teach algebra" and "Space shuttle photos to teach about engineering and geography." And they listened to presenters enumerate the many supposed benefits of computers in the classroom, including preparing students for the twenty-first century workplace, providing access to courses not available locally, and building on the learning styles of kids growing up in a media-saturated world. Vito DiCesare, superintendent of the Beacon school district, was enthusiastic about what he heard, as were other administrators. Instructional computing, he claimed, would close "the gap between richer and poorer school districts."[43]

For more than 100 years, each new development in media-related technology has been greeted with exaggerated expectations for its educational benefits. At the advent of correspondence courses in the 1880s, it was predicted, "The day is coming when the work done by correspondence will be greater in amount than that done in the classroom of our academies and colleges, when the students who shall recite by correspondence will far outnumber those who make oral presentations."[44] Thomas Edison made similar claims for movies. In 1922, he declared:

> The motion picture is destined to revolutionize our educational system and . . . in a few years it will supplant largely, if not entirely, the use of textbooks. I should say that on average we get two percent efficiency out of

schoolbooks as they are written today. The education of the future, as I
see it, will be conducted through the medium of the motion picture . . .
where it should be possible to obtain one hundred percent efficiency."[45]

High hopes accompanied the introduction of instructional radio as well.
"The time may come," the director of the Ohio School of the Air said in
1945, "when a portable radio receiver may be as common in the classroom as is the blackboard."[46] By the 1950s, the hopes had shifted to the
promise of instructional television. But 20 years later, and despite more
than $100 million having been spent on equipment and programming,
teachers reported that they used television during only 2 to 4 percent of
classroom time.[47]

Claims about the educational value of computers have already begun
to be disproved. One emerging concern is the high dropout rate for online courses. Florida Virtual High School had 26 students drop out for
every 100 students who enrolled in an online course. Another school,
Apex, launched with tens of millions of dollars from private investors,
also experienced an unexpectedly high number of dropouts. Of 600 students in 28 states who took online AP courses from Apex in 1999–2000,
two-thirds didn't complete enough work to take an AP exam.[48] Such figures have led researchers to conclude that "students must have a higher-
than-average degree of motivation to succeed in online courses."[49] This
means that instead of serving the often overlooked average student, as
predicted in the utopian rhetoric of conference presenters, online
courses will primarily serve honors students, as almost everything else in
the educational system does.

Also open to question is the widely accepted idea that today's kids,
having grown up with Gameboys, DVD players, the Internet, and cell
phones, are well suited to "computer-mediated learning." The latest scientific findings suggest that the human brain was never designed for the
demands of modern technology—for "rush-rush, multitasking, socially
disconnected 21st-century American life." Neurologist Richard Restak
has argued that this incompatibility contributes to anxiety, depression,
and attention deficit disorder, among other ills. "We've got to rediscover
silence," Restak said.[50]

Gregg D. Jacobs, an assistant professor at Harvard who has worked in
mind-body medicine for 25 years, agrees. He proposes that we get "at

least some of the exposure to solitude, natural settings, and physical activities" that our ancient ancestors did. "Those kinds of things are not
only wired into the brain," he said, "but necessary for health, and we're
deprived of them today."[51] Given that thousands of kids attend school
zonked out on medication for emotional or behavioral disorders, perhaps the classroom should be more a refuge from, and less a replica of,
America's increasingly jarring technoculture.

Some might object that this would interfere with another supposed
benefit of classroom computers, "preparing 21st-century students for
fluent use of interactive media in knowledge-based workplaces."[52] To
which I would reply, "Good!" Underlying the support for instructional
computing is the assumption that keeping up with technology will allow
us to maintain our economic edge, our buy-whatever-we-see-advertised
lifestyle. But is continuing our raging rates of production and consumption actually desirable? For all those who would benefit from it, how
many others would suffer exploitation? Could it even be done without
causing irreparable damage to the planet? Although we may try to ignore them, the signs are unmistakable that the environment is already
seriously stressed. Some New England ponds haven't frozen in 20 years
because of global warming, and a 7,000 square mile "dead zone" of oxy-
genless water stretches from the mouth of the Mississippi River each
summer.[53]

The deeper computers are integrated in the classroom, the deeper
kids are indoctrinated in the cultural belief that technological advances automatically bring economic and other kinds of blessings. But
kids don't need their faith in technology reinforced at school. What
they do need is help reflecting on the implications of technology for
the environment and human health and happiness. And unless they
get it, they may inherit a future as black and sharply pointed as the
Wicked Witch's hat.

It isn't only the physical environment that is in danger of being degraded by technology; the learning environment is also endangered.[54]
Proponents of instructional computing apparently want to "teacher-
proof" the classroom to the greatest extent possible.[55] They seem not to
trust teachers to carry out reforms as mandated or curriculum as designed. There is also the further benefit for administrators and school
boards that they don't have to collective bargain with computers.

I sometimes wonder in what ways technology might have improved the teaching of the legendary sages of old.[56] Would Socrates' dialogs, for example, have been more profound if delivered in the form of Power Point presentations? Would Hillel's aphorisms have been more effective if posted online? Somehow I doubt it. The key element in teaching has always been caring—teacher for student, student for teacher, and both for the subject—and that can't be simulated by any computer software program yet developed.

Instead of focusing on teaching students *through* media-related technologies, perhaps schools should be focusing on teaching them *about* the media. Children's involvement with the media, particularly television, begins early and grows steadily. The average American one-year-old watches six hours of television per week. Two-thirds of children eight and older and one-third of preschoolers have a television in their bedrooms. The average child spends 900 hours per year in school, but 1,023 hours per year watching television. Children eight and older spend the equivalent of a full work week—about seven hours per day—in front of a screen of some kind of electronic media.[57]

Advertisers are well aware how much kids are watching. More than $2 billion is spent annually on advertising targeted at children, 20 times the amount spent just 10 years ago.[58] Between the ages of three and 18, the average child will see about 500,000 television commercials, a number that caused one cultural observer to remark that "the television commercial is the single most substantial source of values to which the young are exposed."[59]

Anxiety that mass media culture has superseded "the role of schools" as "a socializing influence" on children, "shaping their values, beliefs, and habits of mind," has made media literacy a priority in Canada, Australia, the United Kingdom, and other Western nations.[60] Almost every Canadian province has mandated media literacy education for both elementary and secondary students. The Ontario Ministry of Education, the first to do so, offered a definition of media literacy in 1989 that is still widely followed:

> Media literacy is concerned with helping students develop an informed and critical understanding of the nature of mass media, the techniques used by the media and the impact of these techniques. More specifically,

it is education that aims to increase students' understanding and enjoyment of how the media work, how they produce meaning, how they are organized, and how they construct reality. Media literacy also aims to provide students with the ability to create media products.[61]

Teaching students to be more critical of the media may be standard classroom practice in Canada, but the United States ranks "dead last" among developed nations in incorporating media literacy across the curriculum.[62] And this isn't because there aren't any good ideas around for how to incorporate it. Project Look Sharp lists many on its Web site, hosted by Ithaca College. High school math students, the site suggests, might analyze the television Nielsen ratings or survey people about their TV viewing and compute the results. In science, students might "conduct chemical analyses of products advertised in the media (food, vitamins, soda, drugs)."[63] There are similar ideas posted for other subjects and all grades.

As important as analysis is in media literacy education, so is practice. Books such as Steven Goodman's *Teaching Youth Media* and Kathleen Tyner's *Literacy in a Digital World* are filled with advice for teachers interested in having students create their own media products. The premise is that in editing a magazine or shooting a video, students can see for themselves "the multiple layers of data that make up the television or videos they watch and the magazines they read." They can begin to understand "how words can be deleted or added to sentences and made to seem as if they had been originally spoken that way; how causes and effects can be made into their opposite; how perceptions of time, space, power, and history can all be altered without seeming to be"—in sum, how the media can act as "a frame and a filter on the world" while "appearing to be a clear window."[64]

If it isn't a lack of ideas or precedents that is holding up the adoption of media literacy education in the United States, then what is? Researchers have identified at least three factors as necessary for the adoption of new curriculum:

1. Commitment by state school officials.
2. The production and marketing of instructional material by major textbook publishers.

3. The initiation of pre-service and in-service instructional support by teacher education institutions.[65]

None of these is present or forthcoming in relation to media literacy. State school officials, major textbook publishers, and teacher education institutions are all too busy trying to meet—or cash in on—the requirements of the NCLB. When they think about technology, they don't think about using it to teach students to deconstruct, resist, or create alternatives to the bright and bouncy falsehoods of TV commercials or the bright and bloody graphics of violent video games. They think about using it to construct standardized tests or collect and analyze test data. In fact, the latest catchphrase in educational circles is "data mining." Teachers are expected to become "data miners," able to use computers to dig out information as to which of their students got which test questions wrong.[66]

Scarecrow would be disappointed with the direction that education is taking. He didn't want brains so he could pass a standardized test or even get a good job. He wanted brains so he could understand more, enjoy more, help others more—so he could live more fully and connectedly. Unlike many of us, Scarecrow realized right from the start that the most important thing isn't what kind of living you make, but what kind of life.

NOTES

1. Jaime Escalante, "Preparing Students for the World," in *The Crisis of Care*, ed. Susan S. Phillips and Patricia Benner (Washington, D.C.: Georgetown University Press, 1994), 97.

2. Richard L. Curwin and Allen N. Mendler, *As Tough as Necessary* (Alexandria, Va.: Association for Supervision and Curriculum Development, 1997), 5.

3. Noel Langley, Florence Ryerson, and Edgar Allan Woolf, *The Wizard of Oz: The Screenplay*, ed. Michael Patrick Hearn (New York: Delta, 1989), 67.

4. Langley et al., *Wizard*, 67–68.

5. Quoted in William K. Frankena, *Three Historical Philosophies of Education* (Chicago: Scott Foresman, 1965), 69.

6. "2nd Grade Reading Goals," Presentation to the Highland (N.Y.) Board of Education, February 18, 2003, unpaged photocopy.

7. Langley et al., *Wizard*, 68.

8. "2nd Grade Reading Goals."

9. Robert M. Hutchins, *The Conflict in Education in a Democratic Society* (New York: Harper and Brothers, 1953), 14.

10. Langley et al., *Wizard*, 68.

11. Kathleen Vail, "Students Lack the 'Write Stuff,'" *American School Board Journal*, July 2003, 8.

12. Vail, "Students Lack the 'Write Stuff.'"

13. Bruce Springsteen, "No Surrender," in *Songs* (New York: Avon, 1998), 176; Fred Goodman, *The Mansion on the Hill* (New York: Vintage, 1998), 259.

14. "How Schools Fail Our Kids," *District Administration*, May 2003, 15.

15. Meredith Maran, *Class Dismissed* (New York: St. Martin's Press, 2000), 30, 93, 96.

16. Peter Berger, "Rubrics: The Soft Underbelly of Standards," *On Board*, January 13, 2003, 4.

17. State Aid Work Group, *State Aid and Improving Student Achievement in Difficult Times* (Albany: New York Education Department, December 2002), 2, 3, 6.

18. State Aid Work Group, *State Aid*, 6.

19. State Aid Work Group, *State Aid*, 7–8; Maran, *Class Dismissed*, 96.

20. "High-stakes Testing Counterproductive, Studies Suggest," *School Board News*, January 14, 2003, 3.

21. "High-stakes Testing."

22. Deborah Meier, *In Schools We Trust* (Boston: Beacon Press, 2002), 104.

23. Quoted in Alfie Kohn, *The Schools Our Children Deserve* (Boston: Houghton Mifflin, 1999), 78.

24. Susan Ohanian. *One Size Fits Few* (Portsmouth, N.H.: Heinemann, 1999), 12.

25. Denise Clark Pope, *"Doing School"* (New Haven, Conn.: Yale University Press, 2001), 4–5.

26. Pope, *"Doing School,"* 37, 154.

27. Quoted in Kohn, *Schools Our Children Deserve*, 66.

28. John Dewey, *The School and Society*, in *Dewey on Education: Selections*, ed. Martin S. Dworkin (New York: Teachers College Press, 1959), 40.

29. Jerome Bruner, "After John Dewey, What?" in *On Knowing* (Cambridge, Mass.: Belknap Press, 1979), 123.

30. Kohn, *Schools Our Children Deserve*, 55.

31. Langley et al., *Wizard*, 123.

32. Langley et al., *Wizard*, 66.

33. Langley et al., *Wizard*, 70–71, 89, 110, 113, 116.

34. Kohn, *Schools Our Children Deserve*, 503.

35. Maran, *Class Dismissed*, 289.

36. Ellen J. Langer, *The Power of Mindful Learning* (Reading, Mass.: Addison-Wesley, 1997), 2–3.

37. Langer, *The Power*, 4, 121.

38. Kohn, *Schools Our Children Deserve*, 141.

39. Quoted in Neil Postman, *The End of Education* (New York: Knopf, 1996), 94.

40. Associated Press, "School Boards Now Open to Students," *Poughkeepsie Journal*, August 10, 2003, 7A.

41. Jerome Bruner, *The Culture of Education* (Cambridge, Mass.: Harvard University Press, 1996), 39.

42. Langely et al., *Wizard*, 126.

43. Erikah Haavie, "Small City School District Leaders Talk Technology," *Poughkeepsie Journal*, August 12, 2003, 1B.

44. Quoted in Andrew Zucker and Robert Kozma, *The Virtual High School* (New York: Teachers College Press, 2003), 2.

45. Steven Goodman, *Teaching Youth Media* (New York: Teachers College Press, 2003), 11.

46. Quoted in Goodman, *Teaching Youth Media*.

47. Goodman, *Teaching Youth Media*.

48. Zucker and Kozma, *Virtual High School*, 109–11.

49. Zucker and Kozma, *Virtual High School*, 111.

50. Carey Goldberg, "Modern Life Demands Our Divided Attention," *Boston Globe*, July 8, 2003, C3.

51. Quoted in Goldberg, C4.

52. Chris Dede, "Foreword" to *Virtual High School*, vii.

53. See C. A. Bower, *Let Them Eat Data* (Athens: University of Georgia Press, 2000), for a comprehensive analysis of the negative ecological implications of educational computing.

54. Bower, *Let Them Eat Data*, 122.

55. Zucker and Kozma, *Virtual High School*, 13.

56. For a fuller treatment of this idea, see the chapter "The Age of Impatience" in my book *Educated Guess: A School Board Member Reflects* (Lanham, Md.: Scarecrow Education, 2003), 65–67.

57. Margaret Talbot, "Turned On, Tuned Out," *New York Times Sunday Magazine*, February 16, 2003, 9; Goodman, *Teaching Youth Media*, 2–3.

58. Goodman, *Teaching Youth Media*, 6.

59. Postman, *The End of Education*, 33.

60. Goodman, *Teaching Youth Media*, 10.

61. "What Is Media Literacy? A Canadian Definition," Center for Media Literacy, www.medialit.org/reading_room/article176.html (accessed August 18, 2003).

62. Kathleen Tyner, *Literacy in a Digital World* (Mahwah, N.J.: Lawrence Erlbaum, 1998), 130.

63. "Ideas for Incorporating Media Literacy Strategies for High School Grades," Project Look Sharp, www.ithaca.edu/looksharp/resources/integration/highschool (accessed August 18, 2003).

64. Goodman, *Teaching Youth Media*, 6.

65. Tyner, *Literacy in a Digital World*, 137.

66. Kathleen Vail, "School Technology Grows Up," *American School Board Journal*, September 2003, 35–36.

3

HEART

One scene in the novel *The Wizard of Oz* that was omitted from the movie version is a debate between Scarecrow and Tin Man about which is better to have, a brain or a heart. Scarecrow never had either, but Tin Man once had both. He had been fully human until the Wicked Witch of the East enchanted his axe. After that, his axe kept slipping, cutting off first his legs, then his arms, next his head, and finally his torso. The tinsmith who replaced each part in turn forgot, unfortunately, to put brains in Tin Man's head or a heart in his chest. But it was a heart that Tin Man missed the most. "While I was in love [with a Munchkin girl] I was the happiest man on earth;" he says, "but no one can love who has not a heart, and so I am resolved to ask Oz to give me one."[1]

Scarecrow, though similarly deprived, still plans to ask for brains instead of a heart, claiming that "a fool would not know what to do with a heart if he had one." But Tin Man continues to insist, "I shall take the heart, for brains do not make one happy, and happiness is the best thing in the world."[2]

Dorothy doesn't say anything throughout this exchange, as "she is puzzled to know which of her two friends was right."[3] She isn't the only one. Scarecrow and Tin Man express the traditional conflict in Western culture between mind and body, reason and emotion, technology and nature.

Schools increasingly privilege technology over nature—or, in Oz terms, brains over heart—reflecting the priorities of society as a whole. "The educational establishment is itself now infected with the values of the technological worldview," ecologists Bill Devall and George Sessions pointed out, "from the training of administrators and the rise of huge bureaucracies to the attempt to teach using electronic gadgets and computers whenever possible."[4] The growing importance attached to standardized tests is another sign that schools place primary emphasis on filling brains, not on sensitizing or enlarging hearts.

Yet which is needed more? "When we look at the world as it is today," educator Nel Noddings said, "we might well wonder why learning to care is not at the heart of the school curriculum."[5] Susan Ohanian, one of the fiercest critics of the standards movement, agrees. "I can't think of a skill in which I put higher value than learning kindness," she wrote. "I'm not talking of some paltry thing, as my former school district puts it in its wacko language arts standards, *mastering etiquette*; I'm talking about the ability to put yourself in someone else's shoes, the ability to reach out to people and touch their lives, the ability to care for them."[6]

Philosophers and psychologists have variously called this ability empathy, sympathy, altruism, compassion, mercy, pity, and tenderness.[7] Or, as Susan Verducci wryly observed, "Your empathy may be my sympathy."[8] But whatever it is called, the ability to feel with and for others is widely recognized as the "very foundation of morality."[9] Where there is no fellow feeling, there is little, if any, chance of kindness or cooperation. Instead, there is competition and collision and the jagged wounds they leave.

As a general rule, education not only fails to nurture kindness in students, but actually instills its opposite. "A dozen years of schooling often do nothing to promote generosity or a commitment to the welfare of others," school reformer Alfie Kohn said. "To the contrary students are graduated who think being smart means looking out for number one."[10] Devall and Sessions, who embrace a "deep ecology sense of self," an "identification which goes beyond the human to include the nonhuman world," remarked how schools are teaching that "it is 'rational' to compromise on all issues, and that Nature exists as but a commodity to be enjoyed and consumed by humans. . . . Education is preparing young people," they added, "for careers in the highly exploitative, ecologically disastrous technological society."[11]

Perhaps education should be preparing young people instead to live empathetically. Given the tenuousness of modern existence—the wars, the poverty, the pollution—empathy is a basic survival skill. Unless students learn empathetic respect for others, including plants and animals, it seems unlikely that religious and ethnic conflicts will ever be resolved or the natural world healed.

That is why I was disappointed when, on March 5, 2003, no students in my school district walked out of class as part of a worldwide protest against an impending war with Iraq. In a neighboring district, about 50 students, some as young as 12, participated in the "Books Not Bombs" protest. Ironically, the superintendent there disciplined the students for cutting class instead of congratulating them for caring about something else besides grades, clothes, or zits.[12] It is yet another instance of what Alice Miller dubbed "poisonous pedagogy"—pedagogy that fills the needs of adults, not of children.[13] Too often being "good" in school is more about obeying the rules (or scoring well on tests) than about displaying a conscience. "Raising one's hand, not fidgeting, and staying in line become not merely convenient habits," educator Deborah Meier noted, "but moral imperatives."[14]

Obedience may be a habit suitable to a totalitarian society, but empathy is fundamental to democracy.[15] As Meier said, "Democratic society depends on our openness to other ideas, our willingness to suspend belief long enough to entertain ideas contrary to our own."[16] Imagine if anti-abortion activists would even briefly take the perspective of a teen mom, or pro-choicers that of a devout Catholic. It wouldn't necessarily mean there would be agreement about what public policy should be; it would probably mean, though, that there wouldn't be so much anger and suspicion in the face of disagreement.

Tin Man senses that the more empathetic we are, the more human we become. In his section of the song "If I Only Had a Brain/Heart/Nerve," he is "presumin'" he could be "kind-a human" if he only had a heart.[17] The lyrics imply that the distinguishing characteristic of humanity isn't logic or reason, but tenderheartedness. Humans are, in fact, the only primates to shed tears when they cry.[18] And Tin Man cries quite a lot. He cries when Dorothy faints dead away in the poppy field and again when she is imprisoned in the Witch's castle and finally when she is about to leave Oz for home. At one point, Tin Man cries so hard that Scarecrow must warn him, "Don't cry—you'll rust yourself again."[19]

Is the heart, then, simply a soppy sponge? Tin Man sings he would be "tender" and "gentle" and "awful sentimental regarding love and art" if he only had a heart. But he also sings he would be "friends with the sparrows," not just with "the boy that shoots the arrows."[20] That is, empathy comes in a variety of forms and takes many objects: the self, other humans, ideas, the environment.

The Wizard may refer to Tin Man in a fit of pique as "You clinking, clanking, clattering collection of caliginous junk," but that is judging him by appearance only.[21] Despite looking like a robot—his costume was actually made of buckram covered with leather that had been painted silver[22]—Tin Man is more man than machine. His preference for a heart over brains suggests the validity of Charles E. Silberman's observation that "thinking alone does not make a human being human."[23] Nor, ultimately, does it make a student educated. As Aristotle said long ago, and we seem to keep forgetting, "Educating the mind without educating the heart is no education at all."

SHOT THROUGH THE HEART

How can we teach children to care when society treats so many of them uncaringly? According to *The State of America's Children Yearbook*:

- One in three will be poor at some point in his or her childhood.
- One in five was born poor.
- One in six is poor now.
- One in seven has no health insurance.
- One in eight never graduates high school.
- One in 12 has a disability.
- One in 13 was born with low birthweight.
- One in 15 lives at less than half the poverty level.
- One in 24 lives with neither parent.
- One in 26 is born to a mother who received late or no prenatal care.
- One in 60 sees his or her parents divorce in any given year.
- One in 139 will die before his or her first birthday.
- One in 1,056 will be killed by guns before age 20.[24]

Perhaps Susan Ohanian came closest to a comprehensive explanation for these sad statistics when she said, "Nobody gets rich worrying about the children."[25]

School, which you would expect to be a place of refuge for children, a caring environment that promotes social bonding, too often isn't. One-third of the nation's schools, attended by some 14 million students, need extensive repair.[26] Pearl M. Oliner and Samuel P. Oliner noted that only fences and guards can keep children from damaging such schools further. Why? Because children who sit in crowded, crumbling classrooms eventually realize how little others care about them and lash back.[27]

Even in schools without leaky roofs or security bars on the windows, the atmosphere can be toxic. Deborah Meier, who has run experimental schools in New York City and Boston, proposed that children be educated for empathy by extending "kindergarten-like features" throughout the school years. Now, of course, the older children get, the barer education becomes. "As children move up the grades," Meier pointed out, "they are more and more judged in competition with one another, and displays of generosity and affection are increasingly seen as divisive and inappropriate."[28]

Teachers do little to counteract this. Perhaps they haven't received the proper training, or have felt pressured to focus exclusively on academics, or have just been worn down. Rick Weissbourd, a lecturer at the Harvard University Graduate School of Education, found in his research that "disillusionment and depression undermine large numbers of teachers," particularly in urban schools. "They can't get textbooks and other materials," he wrote; "they feel stranded, marooned in their classrooms; they don't get adequate support from administrators; they don't believe that they have the skills to deal with the problems that they confront every day," from drugs in the schoolyard to sex in the stairwells to violence in the halls.[29]

Studies show that depressed adults tend to be withdrawn, irritable, critical, and peremptory. They are generally occupied with their own moods and needs, not those of others. If Weissbourd is right, and many teachers do suffer from a form of depression, then what they find hard to express are exactly the qualities of heart that contribute to caring schools.[30]

None of my four children ever woke up looking forward to another day of school, and why would they, when all that awaited them was more of the same relentless, rule-bound drudgery? The typical American school treats students as products to be pumped out on a fixed schedule, to standard specifications, at the least possible expense. But students aren't products. They are people, distinct individuals who need the sympathy and care of the adults with whom they interact—for example, teachers—if they are to become caring, sympathetic adults in turn.

Jaime Escalante, the math teacher who was the subject of the movie *Stand and Deliver*, shared a story that highlights the importance of teachers making students feel loved and valued. A fellow teacher had two boys named Johnny in his class. One Johnny was an excellent student, the other a goof-off. The teacher suspected that the second Johnny would be a problem all year. Toward the end of September, the school held an open house. A mother came up to the teacher and asked, "How's my Johnny getting along?" For some reason, the teacher assumed that she was the good Johnny's mother. "I can't tell you how much I enjoy him," he said. "I'm glad he's in my class." The next morning, the problem Johnny approached the teacher and said, "My mom told me what you said about me last night. I didn't know any teacher ever wanted me." That day, the problem Johnny did his classwork. The following day, he brought in his homework. Eventually, he became a good friend of the teacher and one of the best students in the class.[31]

The moral of the story, Escalante said, is: "We must not lose hope in our students, and we need to encourage them not to lose hope in themselves."[32] This is certainly true. But the story also illustrates a darker truth: that once a student is labeled dumb or difficult or just average, only an accident of fate can save him or her from the stigma of the label, the feeling of being unwanted, devalued, incarcerated.

My old teachers would be flummoxed to learn that I went on to earn a Ph.D., write books, and become president of a school board. They never had a very high opinion of my abilities, and they let me know it—not only by my grades, but also by contemptuous looks and impatient gestures. I attended public school back in the days when teachers ran their classrooms something like Soviet labor camps of the Stalinist era. They tyrannized us and ridiculed us; at times, they even hit us. They said they were doing this for our own good, and perhaps some actually believed they were. Adults leave the world of childhood so far behind that they quite forget what it is like to be a child, how lonely it can be and how scary.

I ended up hating school. I hated the rules we had to obey and the homework we had to do and the creepy teachers we had to endure, whether cadaverous Mrs. Zack, with her batlike screeching, or stubby, sadistic Mr. Pitti, with his penchant for pinching and twisting the ears of us boys. What I needed, they couldn't give me, and what they gave me, I didn't need.

From remarks my children make at the dinner table, I can tell that school hasn't changed a lot since then. Teachers may not smack students anymore, but they still punish them for trivial offenses and still call them names, still treat them as if they were unfeeling objects. "The most deadly of all possible sins," psychoanalyst Erik Erikson said, "is the mutilation of a child's spirit."[33] As in some vast, never-ending horror movie, children all over the country are going into schools with their spirits more or less intact and coming out with them slashed and bleeding.

Tin Man survived mutilation, largely by taking prosthetics to a whole new level, but also by staying true to his quest for a heart. Our own survival as a society and even a species may well depend on putting, in Anna E. Richert's words, "the heart back into schooling."[34] Teachers must realize that they teach much more than math, English, or history. They teach values—or the lack thereof—by the way they talk to children and each other and by the kinds of behavior they reward and the kinds they punish. Alice Miller, who studied the traditional authoritarian upbringings of the leading figures of the Third Reich, concluded, "Children who are lectured to, learn how to lecture; if they are admonished, they learn how to admonish; if scolded, they learn how to scold; if ridiculed, they learn how to ridicule; if humiliated, they learn how to humiliate; if their psyche is killed, they will kill—the only question is who will be killed: oneself, others, or both."[35] But, by the same token, if children are cared for, there is a pretty good chance that they will learn how to care.

HEART CONDITION

Like a growing number of school districts, the district where I was a board member has a character education program. Ours, which focuses on the hormone-saturated middle school, probably about as close to a land of Oz as you are liable to find this side of the rainbow, is called Project Wisdom. It is organized around monthly themes. March's theme, for example, was "Making Responsible Choices."

Project Wisdom takes a two-prong approach to character education. One prong consists of what some experts categorize as "cheerleading."[36] It involves using colorful banners, posters, and bulletin boards to tout particular ethical values, such as honesty and respect; having the principal recite an inspirational story, poem, or quotation ("Hope is the mother of success."—Samuel Smiles) over the PA system every morning; and holding motivational assemblies.

The second prong relies on positive reinforcement, or what is called "praise and reward."[37] Students "caught" being good receive coupons that they can exchange for privileges or prizes—say, a free ice cream. There are also awards assemblies, where a few selected students are recognized for their exceptional kindness or courtesy.

Does any of this actually work? I suppose it depends on what you mean by "work." If you mean that it helps control students, makes them more respectful of school rules and more obedient to authority, then perhaps it does. At the middle school, discipline referrals were down 20 percent after Project Wisdom had been in effect for a year. But if by "work" you mean that it broadens students, makes them more open-minded and caring, then the results are less impressive.

Darla, my youngest daughter, who entered the middle school simultaneously with Project Wisdom, came home one day with a story that points up the shortcomings of character education of the cheerleading or praise-and-reward variety. She said her seventh-grade English class had read an essay by Chief Dan George about the near extermination of Native Americans by whites. The teacher, hoping to spark discussion, asked for other examples of genocide. "Adolf Hitler killed six million Jews," a student answered. To which a boy in the back added, "Way to go, Adolf!"

It seems unlikely that listening to a poem about brotherhood or attending an assembly on tolerance will resolve this kind of moral insensitivity, which may be more widespread than most of us realize or want to believe. A sixth-grade teacher asked her class, "What's your idea of a beautiful world?" and a boy raised his hand and said, "One without blacks and Jews." An 11th-grade social studies class was discussing the issue of acid rain when a girl referred to environmentalists as "tree huggers" and wondered aloud why they can't all be killed.[38] Such students aren't necessarily from disadvantaged background. Most even get good grades and are considered well adjusted. But they don't have a clue about how to care for others, and they aren't likely to get one from a poster hanging in the cafeteria.

The literature on empathy confirms doubts about the ultimate effectiveness of the cheerleading approach to character education. In the words of one researcher, "Talking about morality, honesty, or kindness in no way ensures that people will act morally, honestly, or kindly."[39] Another noted, "There is little evidence that moralizing to children or giving them direct instruction in moral principles has much effect."[40] Still another reiterated that "neither admonition or exhortation does much to discourage selfishness and promote generosity."[41]

The praise-and-reward approach has also taken its hits. Kathleen Cotton, after an extensive review of the literature, bluntly wrote: "The provision of extrinsic rewards or 'bribes' to improve children's behavior is counterproductive." According to Cotton, "Researchers have found that providing payoffs for prosocial behavior focuses attention on the reward rather than the reason for it and that the desired behaviors tend to lessen or disappear when the reward is withdrawn."[42] One study reported that young children who received frequent praise for displays of generosity—"Good sharing!" or "I'm so proud of you for helping!"— eventually acted less generous on an everyday basis than other children did. They came to see sharing or helping not as something valuable in itself, but as something they had to do to please an adult.[43]

By contrast, researchers have found modeling to be perhaps the most effective means to teach caring. Kathleen A. Brehony explained modeling by drawing an analogy from the animal kingdom: "It is said that when taming and training a wild elephant, the best way to start is by yoking it to one already tamed."[44] The best way to teach caring isn't for significant adults (parents, teachers, coaches, and so on) to tell children to care, but to show them how to care by creating caring relationships with them.

In the early 1970s, the National Institute of Mental Health conducted an experiment in which teachers were either cool or warm toward their students, and either just told them about caring behavior or actually modeled it. The experimenters extrapolated from the findings to child-rearing. Their conclusion:

> The parent who is an altruist in the world but is cold with his child reaps a small harvest in developing altruism in his child. Further, the parent who conveys his values to his child didactically as tidy principles, and no more, accomplishes only that learning in the child. Generalized altruism would appear to be best learned from parents who not only try to inculcate the principles of altruism but who also mainfest altruism in everyday interactions . . . [and whose] practices toward children are consistent with general altruism.[45]

If you require more recent proof of the power of this kind of teaching, then consider Charles Horton, founder of Physicians for Peace. "My parents never sat down and taught me values," he said in an interview; "they just lived them."[46]

Some teachers will object that they haven't the time to model care, that they already have enough to do, what with preparing classes, grading assignments, filling out paperwork, and trying to meet the demand for higher standards. They will say instilling values is a parent's job, not theirs. They will point out that even if they wanted to become more caring teachers, they wouldn't know where to begin, having never been taught caringly themselves back when they were students.

None of which changes the fact that students learn best from those they trust most, and that they will trust most those who show genuine care for them. And how should teachers show care? By attending first to children's needs and only later to lesson plans. By loving children for what they are rather than berating them for what they aren't. By taking children by the hand and going out with them to look, like Tin Man, for a heart in a heartless world.

FROM THE HEART

At one point in Baum's novel, Tin Man is walking down the road with Dorothy, Scarecrow, and Lion when he unintentionally steps on a beetle and kills it. He begins to cry for "the poor little thing," "tears of sorrow and regret" running down his face and rusting the hinges of his jaw.

After he receives several squirts from a handy oilcan, Tin Man says, "This will serve me a lesson to look where I step. For if I should kill another bug or beetle I should surely cry again, and crying rusts my jaw so that I cannot speak." The rest of the day, he walks with his eyes on the ground, and whenever he sees a tiny ant toiling along, he carefully steps over it.[47]

A similar scene was shot for the movie, but it was deleted from the final cut. In the deleted scene, the Witch turns Tin Man into a beehive as punishment for accompanying Dorothy on her quest. A swarm of bees pours out of his mouth, ears, and the funnel in his hat. One bee lands on Dorothy's arm, and Tin Man kills it by accident while brushing it off her. When he realizes what he has done, he sobs, "It's only a man without a heart who could do a thing like that. Poor little bee." Dorothy gets him to stop crying by telling her that it was "just an old drone bee, and it would have died anyway. . . . You put it out of its misery."[48]

Both scenes play up the irony that a man who worries about not having a heart is, of all the characters in *The Wizard of Oz*, the one most capable of sensitivity and kindness. Tin Man operates under the curious delusion that to be anatomically complete or correct is to be morally complete or correct as well. "You people with hearts," he says in the novel, "have something to guide you, and need never do wrong; but I have no heart, and so I must be very careful. When Oz gives me a heart of course I needn't mind so much."[49] Which is precisely the cause of many of the world's problems—people with hearts who forget to use them.

Although Tin Man doesn't know it, he embodies "the deep ecology sense of self" that Bill Devall and George Sessions have advocated. In contrast to the modern Western self, which they define as "an isolated ego striving primarily for hedonistic gratification," the deep ecology sense of self reflects "the realization of 'self-in-Self' where 'Self' stands for organic wholeness." Tin Man cries for the dead beetle in the novel, and the dead bee in the deleted movie scene, because he perceives that there are no boundaries, that everything is interrelated. He seems to understand intuitively a central principle of deep ecology: "if we harm the rest of nature, then we are harming ourselves."[50]

There may be no more important lesson to convey to those growing up in consumer societies, of which the United States is the undisputed world heavyweight champ. "The furnishings of our consumer life-style—things like automobiles, throwaway goods and packaging, a high-fat diet, and air conditioning—can only be provided at great environmental cost," Alan Thein Durning of the Worldwatch Institute pointed out. "Our way of life depends on enormous and continuous inputs of the very commodities that are most damaging to the earth to produce: energy, chemicals, metals, and paper."[51] Unless we ease off on consumption and stop treating nature as something that exists only for our use, we will poison our air and water and unalterably disfigure the land.

Students today do learn in school about acid rain, global warming, and ozone depletion. They do study endangered species and habitat preservation. But, as Nel Noddings said, "the problems they tackle are often focused in faraway places"—the Amazon basin or the Arctic ice cap.[52] Teachers are more comfortable discussing distant environmental issues than ones close to home. As a result, students can participate in numerous activities to save the rainforest but remain ignorant or indifferent about how their own high rate of consumption translates into huge impacts. "By drawing on resources far and near," Durning noted, "consumers cast an ecological shadow over wide regions of the earth."A cute little blouse in the GAP store at the local shopping mall is likely to come from Indonesian oil wells by way of petrochemical plants and textile mills in Singapore and assembly industries in Bangladesh.[53]

So how can we educate students to treat the environment with greater care? How can we instill in them the deep ecology sense of self that Tin Man exemplified when he cried for the dead bugs?[54] How can we get them to conceive of themselves as conservers or even creators rather than consumers?

Devall and Sessions had some suggestions, mostly for high school and college students, though usable with childen in the lower grades, too. They suggested that schools encourage students to create "ectopian visions," "visions that affirm our bonds with Earth." Inspiration for the visions "can be drawn," they said, "from anthropological literature on hunter/gatherers, small-scale agricultural [communities], and contemporary primary cultures." They also compiled a list of questions that could be used to develop ectopian visions: How can humans begin the process of integrating body-mind-spirit? What kinds of social structures are truly sustainable? How can vital needs be defined? How can vital needs be served fully with minimal impact on the requirements of vital needs of nonhumans? Devall and Sessions believed such questions would help students see "viable alternatives to the status quo," which they can then incorporate in their own lives.[55]

Noddings, for her part, emphasized the importance of hands-on learning in raising the ecological consciousness of students. "All schools should have gardens, greenhouses, and window-sill plants," she said.[56] My own experience bears out the value of this. By far my favorite project in grade school was growing Kentucky bluegrass in a shoebox. I still remember my excitement when the grass emerged from the soil with a bluish tint. It was a color I had never seen in grass before.

To this day, I love to grow things, particularly flowers, which light up my yard in the summer like hundreds of birthday candles. Noddings projected that having students clean up streams or plant trees might induce a lifelong commitment to environmental causes, as well as lead some to consider related occupations: horticulture, architectural landscaping, and forestry.[57] But there are other, more immediate reasons to plant. In the words of journalist and avid gardener Ellen Goodman, "Plant, to remember that things do not just appear in the refrigerator. They grow, slowly. Plant, to repair the nearly severed umbilical cord with the natural world. Plant, to keep the pact of mutual caretaking with nature."[58]

Teaching students to act as caretakers won't be easy. Not when the number of shopping malls in the United States has surpassed the number of high schools. And not when Americans go to malls on average once a week—more often than they go to church or synagogue.[59] It can be done, though. There are teachers already doing it, even with young children.

Kate Lyman teaches a combined second- and third-grade class at Hawthorne School in Madison, Wisconsin. She recently put together a whole unit on child labor, a topic she had explored sporadically in the past.[60] Around the world, some 250 million children between the ages of 5 and 14 are forced to work for a living. Lyman wanted her students to develop empathy with the young girls in Guatemala who carry bricks on their heads up steep hills to construction sites; the teenagers in China who assemble toys for 12 hours a day without such basic rights as bathroom privileges or sick leave; the many children in Nepal who spend their childhoods under a hot sun, breaking rocks to make gravel. She also wanted them to think critically about consumerism and how our gains might be other people's losses to reflect, for example, on the plight of China's toy workers the next time they went into a Wal-Mart or Toys 'R' Us to buy Mattel's Barbie or Hasboro's Pokemon.[61] Finally, Lyman wanted the unit to inspire her students to take action.[62] The point of empathy, after all, isn't just to feel something, but to do something positive with the feeling.

Lyman accomplished most of what she hoped she would, and she did it using classroom strategies that years of research have shown to be effective means of fostering empathy and prosocial behavior. The strategies included:

Exposure to emotionally arousing stimuli. Researchers have found that exposure to emotionally arousing stimuli, such as portrayals of misfortune, deprivation, or distress, tends to increase empathy.[63] Lyman had her class watch part of *Zoned for Slavery*, a video in which a reporter sneaks into a maquila, or sweatshop, in Honduras and interviews the girls who sew shirts there. "The students groaned," Lyman recounted, "as they heard that the girls need to pay for their bus transportation and their lunch out of their meager salary." After the video, students shared their feelings. "That's not fair," one said. "They can't even go to the bathroom or get a drink of water." A second said, "We should give money to the poor people so they wouldn't have to work." A third said, "I have an idea. Don't buy any shirts from those companies. Then they won't make so much money!" The momentum of wanting to take action carried into the following weeks, with students writing letters to the editor, the president's wife, and clothing companies protesting child labor.[64]

Role-playing. Activities in which children or adults imagine and act out the role of another enhance empathetic feelings and understanding. Researchers have noted increases in empathy even when children are asked to take the point of view of an animal, plant, or inanimate object.[65] Lyman's students did a role-playing activity in which they were assigned the job of measuring or tying knots in coarse twine, supposedly as part of a rug-making factory. They went about their jobs under strict rules of no talking, no drinks or bathroom breaks, no getting up from their seats, no imperfections. Any violation of the rules reduced their pay (five pennies). After 15 minutes, Lyman called a stop, concerned that students were becoming upset. "That felt real," several said. One guessed, "I bet you were doing this so we could feel how the workers felt." The students had previously read about children in Pakistan who work for three cents a day in carpet factories and, if they protest, are beaten and tied to their chairs.[66]

Sustained practice in imagining another's perspective. For many young people, the ability to imagine another's perspective doesn't come fast, but sustained practice at perspective-taking has been found to increase levels of empathy.[67] Lyman gave her students repeated opportunities to imagine what it would be like to work long hours for low pay under brutal conditions. One day, she passed out copies of photos from *Stolen Dreams*, a book on child workers. She suggested students "describe not only what they saw in the photos, but also what they imagined the children in the photos felt and what their lives were like." The students responded with moving poems, including one about a child construction worker in Kathmandu that began: "She doesn't wear shoes / removes dirt from a hole / carries heavy things / works in the heat / works every day."[68]

There are other proven strategies, some of which Lyman used, that allow teachers to encourage the development of empathy in children. Teachers can focus children's attention on the lives and works of famous empathetic people, such as Florence Nightingale, Albert Schweitzer, Martin Luther King Jr., and Mother Theresa. They can implement cooperative learning, organizing children into groups whose members are different from one another in race, gender, socioeconomic status, and ability level. And they can practice positive trait attribution (also called "dispositional praise")—that is, emphasize to children that positive, pro-social traits are part of their nature. For example, a teacher might say to a child, "I'll bet you shared with Susie because you're a nice person who likes to make other children happy."[69] The "teacher's goal should not be to simply produce a given behavior," Alfie Kohn explained, "but to help that child see himself or herself as the kind of person who is responsible and caring."[70]

Anything that serves to stir, stretch, or strengthen the imagination apparently contributes to making empathy possible. Maxine Greene noted that imagination is "what enables us to cross the empty spaces between ourselves and those we teachers have called 'other' over the years. If those others are willing to give us clues, we can look in some manner through strangers' eyes and hear through their ears."[71] It is the arts in general, and stories in particular, that may provide the best clues. "Part of the great wonder of reading," novelist Anna Quindlen said, "is that it has the ability to make human beings feel connected to one another."[72] Daily, Lyman read stories about working children aloud to her students or had them read such stories silently to themselves. They came away with more than just information about the history of child labor in the United States or the complex interplay nowadays between third-world poverty and corporate profit; they came away with informed hearts.

Toward the end of *The Wizard of Oz*, with Dorothy and her friends gathered to receive their reward for defeating the Wicked Witch, the Wizard hesitates as he is about to give Tin Man a heart—or, rather, a huge heart-shaped watch and chain. "Hearts will never be practical," the Wizard warns, "until they can be made unbreakable."[73] But Tin Man still wants one. Just as he clung to his axe throughout the movie, so he clings to the belief that to have a heart is to have everything worth having. And who are we, tormented by war, poisoned by pollution, dying by the thousands every day in consequence of our own carelessness and cruelty, to doubt that he is right?

NOTES

1. L. Frank Baum, *The Wizard of Oz* (New York: Tor, 1993), 35–36.

2. Baum, *Wizard*, 36.

3. Baum, *Wizard*, 36.

4. Bill Devall and George Sessions, *Deep Ecology* (Salt Lake City: Peregrine Smith, 1985), 183.

5. Nel Noddings, *Educating Moral People* (New York: Teachers College Press, 2002), 32.

6. Susan Ohanian, *One Size Fits Few* (Portsmouth, N.H.: Heinemann, 1999), 130.

7. Daniel C. Batson, "How Social an Animal? The Human Capacity for Caring," *American Psychologist* 45 (March 1990): 339.

8. Susan Verducci, "A Conceptual History of Empathy and a Question It Raises for Moral Education," *Educational Theory* 50 (Winter 2000): 3.

9. Sissela Bok, *Mayhem* (Reading, Mass.: Addison-Wesley, 1998), 38. The word *empathy* comes from the German *Einfuhlung*, which means "feeling into." Frans de Waal, *Good Natured* (Cambridge, Mass.: Harvard Uinversity Press, 1996), 79.

10. Alfie Kohn, "Caring Kids: The Role of Schools," *Phi Delta Kappa* 72, no. 7 (1991): 498.

11. Devall and Sessions, *Deep Ecology*, 67, 182–83.

12. Gabriel J. Wasserman, "Local Students Make Voices Heard on War," *Poughkeepsie Journal*, March 6, 2003, 1A, 6A.

13. Alice Miller, *For Your Own Good*, trans. Hildegarde Hannum and Hunter Hannum (New York: Farrar, Straus and Giroux, 1983), 9.

14. Deborah Meier, "Supposing That . . . ," *Phi Delta Kappan* 78 (December 1996): 271–76.

15. Miller, *For Your Own Good*, 67.

16. Meier, "Supposing," 271–76.

17. Noel Langley, Florence Ryerson, and Edgar Allan Woolf, *The Wizard of Oz: The Screenplay*, ed. Michael Patrick Hearn (New York: Delta, 1989), 74.

18. de Waal, *Good Natured*, 55.

19. Langley et al., *Wizard*, 84.

20. Langley et al., *Wizard*, 74.

21. Langley et al., *Wizard*, 101.

22. Aljean Harmetz, *The Making of The Wizard of Oz* (New York: Limelight, 1977), 171.

23. Charles E. Silberman, *Crisis in the Classroom* (New York: Random House, 1970), 7–8.

24. "The State of America's Children Yearbook 2001: 25 Key Facts about American Children," Children's Defense Fund, www.childrendefense.org (accessed March 5, 2003).

25. Ohanian, *One Size*, 124.

26. These figures, from a 1995 General Accounting Office report, are quoted in Ohanian, *One Size*, 111.

27. Pearl M. Oliner and Samuel P. Oliner, *Toward a Caring Society* (Westport, Conn.: Praeger, 1995), 11–12.

28. Meier, "Supposing," 271–76.

29. Rick Weissbourd, "Moral Teachers, Moral Students," *Educational Leadership* 60 (March 2003): 9.

30. Weissbourd, "Moral Teachers."

31. Jaime Escalante, "Preparing Students for the World," in *The Crisis of Care*, ed. Susan S. Phillips and Patricia Benner (Washington, D.C.: Georgetown University Press, 1994), 100.

32. Escalante, "Preparing Students."

33. Silberman, *Crisis*, 10.

34. Anna E. Richert, "The Corrosion of Care in the Context of School," in *Crisis of Care*, 109.

35. Miller, *For Your Own Good*, 98.

36. Eric Schaps, Esther F. Schaeffer, and Sanford N. McDonnell, "What's Right and Wrong in Character Education Today," *Education Week*, September 12, 2001, 40.

37. Schaps et al., "What's Right."

38. These are actual incidents witnessed by my children and reported to me.

39. Silberman, *Crisis*, 9.

40. Schaps et al., "What's Right," 40.

41. Morton Hunt, *The Compassionate Beast* (New York: William Morrow, 1990), 209.

42. Kathleen Cotton, "Close-Up #13: Developing Empathy in Children and Youth," School Improvement Research Series, NW Regional Education Laboratory, www.nwrel.org/scpd/sirs7/cu13.html (accessed October 30, 2002).

43. Alfie Kohn, "Almost There, but Not Quite," *Educational Leadership* 60 (March 2003): 29.

44. Kathleen A. Brehony, *Ordinary Grace* (New York: Riverhead Books, 1999), 21–22.

45. Hunt, *Compassionate Beast*, 211.

46. Brehony, *Ordinary Grace*, 126.

47. Baum, *Wizard*, 42.

48. Langley et al., *Wizard*, 136.

49. Baum, *Wizard*, 43.

50. Devall and Sessions, *Deep Ecology*, 67–68.

51. Alan Thein Durning, *How Much Is Enough?* (New York: Norton, 1992), 52.

52. Nel Noddings, *The Challenge to Care in Schools* (New York: Teachers College Press, 1992), 135.

53. Durning, *How Much*, 54.

54. Albert Einstein expressed it as well when he spoke about "widening our circle of compassion to embrace all living things and the whole of nature in its beauty." Quoted in Brehony, *Ordinary Grace*, 169.

55. Brehony, *Ordinary Grace*, 163

56. Noddings, *Challenge*, 133.

57. Noddings, *Challenge*, 136

58. Noddings, *Challenge*, 134.

59. Durning, *How Much*, 130–31.

60. Kate Lyman, "Exploring Child Labor with Young Students," Rethinking Schools Online, www.rethinkingschools.org/archive/17_02/Labo172.shtml (accessed January 6, 2003).

61. Robert A. Senser, "Toying with Lives," *American Educator* (Winter 2002): 36, 38.

62. Lyman, "Exploring."

63. Cotton, "Developing Empathy."

64. Lyman, "Exploring."

65. Cotton, "Developing Empathy."

66. Lyman, "Exploring."

67. Cotton, "Developing Empathy."

68. Lyman, "Exploring."

69. Cotton, "Developing Empathy."

70. Kohn, "Caring Kids," 501.

71. Maxine Greene, *Releasing the Imagination* (San Francisco: Jossey-Bass, 1995), 3.

72. Ohanion, *One Size*, 79.

73. Langley et al., *Wizard*, 124.

4

COURAGE

"What makes the sphinx the seventh wonder?" the Cowardly Lion asks in the song "If I Were King of the Forest." "What makes the dawn come up like thunder? What makes the Hottentot so hot? What puts the 'ape' in apricot?" As anyone familiar with *The Wizard of Oz* knows—and who isn't familiar with *The Wizard of Oz*?—the answer to all these questions is "Courage!" It is courage, according to Lion, that "makes a king out of a slave" as well as "makes the flag on the mast to wave."[1]

Yip Harburg, who wrote the lyrics for "If I Were King" and the other songs in *The Wizard of Oz*, once observed: "The process of putting music in [a movie] is very intricate. The function of song is to simplify everything, to take out the clutter of too much plot and too many characters, to telescope everything into one emotional idea."[2] "If I Were King," for all its humor, actually contains a serious point, which is that every person needs some measure of courage in order to be effective. Courage is a so-called "executive virtue," meaning that it enables a person to successfully execute his or her purposes.[3] A person who lacks sufficient courage may be too fearful to act in the first place or, if embarked upon an action, too easily frustrated to finish it.

Some have reckoned courage "the greatest of all virtues," because, as Samuel Johnson explained, "unless a man has that virtue, he has no security for preserving any other."[4] Rushworth M. Kidder and Martha

Bracy, co-authors of "Moral Courage: A White Paper," found courage to be not quite like other virtues, such as honesty, fairness, responsibility, and compassion. "Maybe it's the catalyst that speeds up the reaction times of the others," they wrote. "Maybe it's the hardware upon which the software of the other values operates."[5] Courage apparently doesn't just put "the 'ape' in apricot." It also puts the *vir*—the Latin root of the word *virility*—into virtue.

If courage is, in fact, as admirable a quality as writers contend, then schools should be trying to help students attain it. But how would they do that? What exactly would be taught if schools tried to teach courage?

The curriculum is far from obvious. Although courage has been celebrated in story since ancient times—William Ian Miller estimated that it is "the most frequent theme of all world literature"[6]—no single definition of courage seems to cover all cases. "There are different kinds of examples of acts we consider to be courageous," philosopher Douglas N. Walton noted, "and, as Socrates would have said, we need to know what general principle is common to these examples to really find out what courage is."[7] Is courage a physical feat, a moral trait, or a combination of both? Is courage having the bold determination to attack or the grim fortitude to withstand attack? Is courage acting without fear or acting in spite of fear? Hollywood cowboy John Wayne thought the latter, drawling, "Courage is being scared to death—and saddling up anyway."[8]

As we accompany Lion down the Yellow Brick Road, we will sort through competing ideas about what constitutes courage. We will examine why some now consider physical, or soldierly, courage problematic, and why moral courage seems to be gaining in social importance. We will also examine possible methods for teaching courage—by precept, by studying the lives of heroes, and by practice. Given the complexity of such issues, we may need courage ourselves to see our quest through to the end. If so, let's hope that we, like Lion, can find it.

THE PROBLEM OF PHYSICAL COURAGE

Lion understands courage in physical terms, as a matter of manly strength and energy. His lack of courage makes him not only less of a lion in his own eyes, but also less of a male. As he sets off with Dorothy,

Scarecrow, and Tin Man to see the Wizard, he sings: "Yeah, it's sad, believe me, missy / When you're born to be a sissy, / Without the vim and
verve." He admits that in his cowardly condition, he is "just a dande-
lion," a ludicrous, effeminate creature.[9]

In many cultures, ours included, courage is inseparable from questions of gender.[10] Americans often equate courage with a significant
piece of male anatomy: "balls." We describe the courageous as "ballsy"
and tell the timid to "grow a pair of balls." Lion has, in the vernacular,
"no balls," and the shame of having failed to fulfill his culturally prescribed gender role almost overwhelms him. "Well, wouldn't you feel
degraded to be seen in the company of a cowardly lion?" he asks his
three new acquaintances. "I would."[11]

The very word *courage* reflects a primitive notion of manliness. It de-
rives from the French *coeur*, meaning "heart," though the heart not as the
seat of feeling or sentiment, but as a source of vigorous persistence, power.
A horse's mane and a rooster's comb were once called their "courage" because they were thought to signify aggression and sexual potency.[12]

It is in the form of aggressive, warlike acts that courage has traditionally been celebrated. "Time out of mind," nineteenth-century English
novelist William Makepeace Thackeray said, "strength and courage have
been the theme of bards and romances. I wonder if it is because men
are cowards in heart that they admire bravery so much and place military valor so far beyond every other quality for reward and worship."[13]
Popular culture continues to glamorize the concept of courage as "violent acts of bloodshed perpetrated in rage or revenge"—what Walton
called "the 'Incredible Hulk' reaction."[14] Movies in particular give us heroes with big muscles and bigger guns who move through the world as
through a battlefield, proving their courage by inflicting maximum ca-
sualties on the enemy, be the enemy human, alien, or machine.

But not only Hollywood has associated true courage with behavior in
battle. So have certain philosophers. Aristotle, for example, believed that
the most impressive displays of courage occur where the most impressive
danger of death, pain, and mutilation exists, and that this is in war.[15]

Ironically, generals, who presumably are the real experts in these mat-
ters, can't always agree among themselves what courage is or how it is
best demonstrated. Plato's dialog *Laches* portrays two Athenian generals, Nicias and Laches, as being unable to come up with a satisfactory

definition of courage despite—or perhaps even because of—prodding from Socrates.

Asked by Socrates to define courage, Laches replies, "He is a man of courage who does not run away, but remains at his post and fights against the enemy," which is the traditional idea of manly valor, what the Greeks called *andreia*. Socrates points out, however, that courageous acts aren't limited only to soldiers in battle, for there are also those "who are courageous in perils by sea, and who in disease, or in poverty, or again in politics, are courageous." Thus admonished, Laches makes a second attempt at a definition. Courage, he now says, is "a sort of endurance of the soul." It is a position later contradicted by Nicias, who proposes instead that courage is "a sort of wisdom," "the knowledge of the grounds of hope and fear."[16]

Laches ends inconclusively—the case in many of Plato's dialogs—with Socrates admitting that "we are all in the same perplexity" about what courage is.[17] Scholars have nonetheless argued that the true definition of courage in the dialog lies in combining the definitions of both Laches and Nicias. Courage, by this account, is "a kind of endurance, oriented by the knowledge of what is to be dreaded and dared."[18] But there is reason to doubt whether this is indeed the secret meaning of the dialog. The historical Laches and Nicias, as readers in Plato's time knew, would suffer crushing defeats by the enemies of Athens and be killed in battle, Laches at Mantinea and Nicias in Sicily. If the dialog has a secret meaning, perhaps it is that the soldierly definition of courage is disastrously inadequate.

Socrates seems to say as much by his refusal to acquiesce in it. Although the Athenian military caste conceived of courage as battle-tested toughness, the dialog suggests that persistence in open-ended philosophical inquiry is also a form—perhaps the highest form—of courage. Socrates would eventually swallow poison rather than repudiate philosophy and teaching. His death, theologian Paul Tillich wrote, "brought a profound change in the traditional meaning of courage. . . . Soldierly fortitude was transcended by the courage of wisdom."[19]

In the modern world, the concept of "dauntless, assertive soldier courage" has been steadily eroded by advances in military technology.[20] To soldiers during the American Civil War, courage had a narrow, rigid meaning: "heroic action undertaken without fear."[21] But as technology intensified the destructiveness of war, belief in the efficacy of physical courage decayed. "A courage earlier thought decisive in war as an extension of the will of the individual," historian Gerald F. Lindermann explained, "yielded to the power of the machine gun and a long-range artillery capable of obliterating men and even the landscapes over which they fought."[22] By World War II, Gen. Dwight D. Eisenhower, supreme commander of the Allied Expeditionary Force, would grimly define courage as "the uncomplaining acceptance of unendurable conditions."[23]

If physical courage has become less relevant in times of war, it has become virtually irrelevant in times of peace. "No longer does the mere satisfaction of basic needs entail or require courage," Kidder and Bracy pointed out in their White Paper. "Rarely . . . do we have to think about physically defending ourselves or our loved ones. Where once the frontier loomed mysterious and uncharted, global positioning satellites now take us to our mark."[24] So dull and predictable has life grown in Western societies that people must contrive occasions for courage, from extreme sports and survival treks to high-risk financial ventures.

Philosophy, too, has increasingly raised questions about physical courage. Is this aggressive form of courage a worthy quality? Should it even be tolerated, let alone exalted? Walton, in *Courage: A Philosophical Investigation*, acknowledged that courage has traditionally been defined by violence and bloodshed, but asked, "Is that how a civilized society should define [courage]?" He thought not.[25]

Neither did Amelie O. Rorty, who claimed that courage in its "traditional combative forms" threatens to become excessive and overwhelm other prized goods. The confidence that is a part of courage, she wrote, diminishes the willingness of the courageous to avoid confrontation. "Perceiving actions as victories or defeats, and compromise as partial loss," she said, they "don't usually promote, and often resist, cooperative, compromising attitudes."[26] The result—globally as well as locally—is opposition and conflict.

There is a sense among modern philosophers, then, that if we want to retain courage as a virtue, we need to demilitarize it. Of course, this has its own potential pitfalls. In the process of demilitarizing courage, we may end up trivializing it. Already people talk about having the courage to diet or quit smoking. Shouldn't courage have bigger, nobler objectives in view?

In *The Wizard of Oz*, when Lion, despite confessing fear, helps rescue Dorothy from the Witch's dark castle, he exhibits the strength and daring typically associated with physical courage. What makes his feat admirable, though, isn't that he was strong and brave—tyrants can be strong and brave, terrorists can be strong and brave—but that he was strong and brave in a just cause and from good motives: loyalty, friendship, love. In other words, it wasn't enough for Lion to be courageous; he also had to be moral.

THE LONELINESS OF MORAL COURAGE

The term "moral courage" didn't appear in English until the nineteenth century.[27] Even today, the catalog of the Library of Congress doesn't list one book titled *Moral Courage*.[28] Yet as the visible damage from corporate greed, political lies, and other craven human behavior mounts, there is a growing recognition that moral courage is indispensable to civilized society. "Without it, our brightest virtues rust from lack of use," Kidder and Bracy said. "With it, we build piece by piece a more ethical world."[29]

Victorian philosopher Henry Sidgwick defined moral courage as people "facing the pains and dangers of social disapproval in the performance of what they believe to be duty."[30] Most of those who have since thought about moral courage have agreed with him that it is a lonely kind of courage. The Maine Commission on Ethical and Responsible Student Behavior said moral courage involves doing "the right thing even if it's not popular," while William Ian Miller wrote that it "often requires making a stand, calling attention to yourself, or running the risk of being singled out in an unpleasant and painful way."[31]

Unlike physical courage, which has long been considered the property of men at war, moral courage is available to people of all types and circumstances—students, the old, women. But moral courage isn't only more democratic than physical courage; it is also more appropriate to the modern age, where one is more likely to have to reject evil conformity or defy immoral orders than to engage in hand-to-hand combat. Not that the morally courageous can't still suffer great harm. They may risk their physical well-being, their social standing, their financial prospects, and their relations with colleagues.[32]

The impeachment of President Andrew Johnson in 1868 provides a classic example of moral courage.[33] As the impeachment effort took shape, it became obvious that Johnson wouldn't be able to receive a fair trial. The Radical Republicans in the Senate, angry at his refusal to support their policies, were determined to get him out of the White House on any grounds, real or imagined. They needed only one more vote to convict Johnson, and it belonged to Edmund G. Ross, a young Republican senator from Kansas. The pressure on Ross to vote for impeachment was intense. He was badgered, threatened, offered bribes. But even though he personally disliked Johnson, Ross believed that the executive branch would be compromised if the president was forced to step down from political considerations. And so, when the Chief Justice of the Supreme Court, who was presiding over the trial, called his name, Ross answered, "Not guilty."

Ross's vote against impeachment ended his political career, as he knew it would. "I almost literally looked down into my open grave," he would say years later of the moment he cast his vote.[34] Newspapers denounced him as "a miserable poltroon and traitor," and citizens on the street passed him as if he were "a leper, with averted face and every indication of hatred and disgust."[35] After returning to Kansas in 1871, he and his family suffered social ostracism, physical abuse, and near poverty.

One historian has called Ross's sacrifice "the most heroic act in American history, incomparably more difficult than any deed of valor upon the field of battle."[36] Moral courage is often described through military analogies or images of physical toughness ("standing up," "standing firm," "taking a stand"). William Ian Miller contended that these are more than mere metaphors; they are indications that moral courage "needs enough physical backing not to be deterred from its moral agenda with laughable ease."[37] Socrates' pursuit of philosophical truth took moral courage, and ultimately, when he was faced with prison and death, it took physical courage, too.

So did the actions of "righteous gentiles," the handful of non-Jews who, ignoring the risk to themselves and their families, sheltered Jews from the Nazis during the Holocaust. Cynthia Ozick hailed them as "heroes of our battered world":

What other name can they possibly merit? In the Europe of the most savage decade of the twentieth century not to be a bystander was the choice of an infinitesimal few. These few are more substantial than the multitudes from whom they distinguished themselves; and it is from these undeniably heroic and principled few that we learn the full resonance of civilization.[38]

If the world were a peaceful, unproblematic place, rather than the kind of nightmare Ozick decried, there would be no need for courage. As Walton said, "Courage is a concomitant of the nasty, the awful, and the annoying."[39] The value of courage lies in its power to tilt the world away from evil and toward good; think of Mahatma Gandhi courageously enduring repeated internment to free India from British colonial rule, or of Martin Luther King Jr., courageously standing up to death threats and police dogs to end segregation. The justice and morality so crucial to the survival of civilized society require the existence of such a thing as courage.

But no matter how desirable it may therefore be to teach courage, is it actually possible? No one teaches Lion to have courage. He already possesses it. He just doesn't believe he does, a point made even more clearly in the novel *The Wizard of Oz* than in the movie. When Lion asks the Wizard for courage in the novel, the Wizard answers: "You have plenty of courage, I am sure. . . . All you need is confidence in yourself. There is no living thing that is not afraid when it faces danger. True courage is in facing danger when you are afraid, and that kind of courage you have in plenty."[40] Nonetheless, Lion insists that the Wizard give him "the sort of courage that makes one forget he is afraid." The Wizard complies by bidding Lion to drink the contents of a square green bottle. "How do you feel now?" the Wizard asks. "Full of courage," Lion says.[41]

Of course, this is the power of suggestion at work. The Wizard can't make Lion courageous any more than he can make Scarecrow smart or Tin Man caring. The most the Wizard can do is create opportunities for Lion to be what he should be and position him to seize them. Perhaps that, in the end, is all any teacher can ever do.

"LET'S ROLL"

Some philosophers object to the traditional view of courage as a disposition or trait of character. They see it more as a free-floating virtue that can suddenly appear in anyone. Walton cites the case of a passenger with no flight training who took the controls of a small plane after the pilot had a heart attack. Following instructions over the radio, the passenger landed the plane safely. It didn't matter during the crisis whether he was of low character or had a shady past. What mattered was that when faced with a dangerous situation, he displayed the wit and the will—in Walton's eyes, the courage—to retrieve the situation from disaster.[42]

According to this interpretation, courage just happens. The older, Aristotelian tradition holds that courage is primarily a quality not of individual actions, but of individual character. Another example involving a plane may help clarify the distinction.

On September 11, 2001, four Arab terrorists hijacked United Flight 93 en route from Newark, New Jersey, to San Francisco. Some of the 37 passengers aboard called family members and friends on their cell phones to tell them what had happened and learned in turn that other hijacked planes had crashed that morning into the World Trade Center in New York and the Pentagon in Washington, D.C. Realizing that their plane would also be used as a missile, the passengers decided to fight the hijackers. A GTE-Verizon operator who was in contact during the hijacking with passenger Todd Beamer, an account manager for Oracle software, heard him say to someone else: "You ready? Okay. Let's roll." Then she heard only silence. The plane crashed into a field outside Shanksville, Pennsylvania, rather than hitting its presumed target, a Washington landmark, such as the White House or the Capitol.[43]

Beamer's words, "Let's roll," came to embody the courage of those on Flight 93. Although it was impossible to reconstruct from the cockpit voice recorder exactly what happened in the final moments of the flight, it does appear that the passengers acted with heroic purpose. Jack Grandiolas, whose wife, Lauren, died in the crash, expressed the popular perception when he said:

> They were the ultimate patriots. They did the most democratic thing they could do. They gathered information, they did reconnaissance, they voted to do something. They were ordinary citizens thrown into a combat situation. No one was a general or a dictator. Their first thought was to be selfless. They knew, "There's a 98 percent chance we're not going to make it, but let's save others." That's what Americans are about.[44]

But *New York Times* reporter Jere Longman, in researching his book about Flight 93, *Among the Heroes,* found that the passengers weren't "ordinary citizens placed in an extraordinary situation," as they had often been portrayed.[45] Rather, they were "people on top of their game, who kept score in their lives and who became successful precisely because they were assertive and knew how to make a plan and carry it out."[46] Their courage wasn't a function of the moment, but of long-standing character traits. The mother of one passenger said of her son, "He had a very strong sense of what the right course in life was."[47] The teacher of another passenger said, "She was the kind of person who faced internal struggles and was always trying to do what was right, what had to be done."[48] The friend of still another said, "Alan just went for things. He knew courage was very necessary for a life fully lived."[49]

The more one learns about the people on Flight 93, the more valid the Aristotelian view of the connection between character and courage seems. Passenger Tom Burnett, chief operating officer of Thoratic, a company that manufactures medical devices, adorned his office with busts of Abraham Lincoln, Theodore Roosevelt, and Winston Churchill, "strong leaders who had acted decisively and according to their consciences in times of crisis, even in the face of public opposition."[50] Another passenger, Jeremy Glick, was a former national collegiate judo champion who enjoyed reading the work of Transcendentalist essayist and poet Ralph Waldo Emerson, after whom he named his daughter.[51]

If courage depends on character, as these brief profiles suggest, and character can be instilled, as philosophers and educators claim, then courage can, in fact, be taught. It can be taught chiefly through precept, example, and practice.[52] Each method may be especially appropriate for specific grade levels.[53]

The use of precepts seems best suited to children of primary school age, who are still acquiring the basics of good character and aren't capable yet of sophisticated moral reflection. Ethicist Joel J. Kupperman pointed out that moral reflection can take place only after students have absorbed central moral norms, which are perhaps most memorably conveyed in the form of precepts—that is, as rules, maxims, sayings. "To suppose," he wrote, "that there can be effective moral reflection without a first stage in which categories are learned and habits and attitudes are formed is as naive in its way as to suppose that secondary-school mathematics can be taught effectively to girls and boys who have never learned number concepts."[54]

There are many precepts available to instruct young students in courage and help them distinguish it from cowardice. The sources of the precepts range across centuries and cultures:

Confucius: "To know what is right and not do it is the worst cowardice."

Shakespeare: "Cowards die many times before their deaths; / The valiant never taste of death but once."

Andrew Jackson: "One man with courage makes a majority."

Babe Ruth: "Never let the fear of striking out get in your way."[55]

Teachers might follow up such sayings by engaging students in conversations about why courage is important, what circumstances require it, and who qualifies in their minds as courageous. After all, direct instruction—or, in Nel Noddings' disparaging term, "indoctrination"—isn't likely to nurture the kind of morally and intellectually courageous people that a democracy needs; open discussion is.[56]

Older students, roughly those in secondary school, would presumably benefit more from studying historical and other examples (novels, films, plays) of courageous actions. John F. Kennedy concluded his Pulitzer Prize–winning *Profiles in Courage*, which recounted the self-sacrifice of eight politicians who took unpopular stands, by asserting: "The stories of past courage can define that ingredient—they can teach, they can offer hope, they can provide inspiration."[57]Although not included in Kennedy's book, one story that seems well worth sharing with students old enough to tolerate moral complexity is that of John Adams's defense of the British soldiers and their officer indicted in the Boston Massacre of March 5, 1770.

Adams, then 34 years old, took the case after no other lawyer would.[58] Taking the case, he felt, was his duty, not only as a lawyer, but also as a patriot. He believed that no one in a free country—not even redcoats who had suddenly opened fire on a crowd, killing five men—should be denied the right to counsel and a fair trial. Such was the mood in Boston, though, that he couldn't help worrying about his family's safety as well as his own. For reassurance, he copied into his diary a line from a treatise by the Italian penologist Cesare, Marchese di Beccaria: "If, by supporting the rights of mankind, and of invincible truth, I shall contribute to save from the agonies of death one unfortunate victim of tyranny, or, of ignorance, equally fatal, his blessings and years of transport will be sufficient consolation to me for the contempt of all mankind."[59]

Over two trials, Adams won the acquittal of the officer and six of the eight soldiers (the other two were found guilty of manslaughter, for which they were branded on their thumbs). The public reacted angrily to the verdicts. Adams was denounced in the *Boston Gazette* and suffered the loss of more than half his law practice. Years later, he would recall it as the most exhausting case he ever undertook, but would add with justifiable pride that it was also "one of the most gallant, generous, manly and disinterested actions of my whole life, and one of the best pieces of service I ever rendered my country."[60]

The story dramatizes just the kind of courage that one hopes students would learn to emulate. Most stories circulating in American popular culture glorify violent displays of physical courage, but members of a democratic society need something more than an appetite for bloodshed. They need the courage to question the authority of popular opinion. They need the courage to live with open-endedness. They need the courage to bear the discomfort and stress that pursuing the Socratic path often brings.

Theologian Martin Buber told a gathering of teachers in 1939—the year of the Nazi blitzkrieg—that it was their job to awaken in students moral courage, "the courage to shoulder life again." They could do that, he said, by putting before their students "the image of a great character who denies no answer to life and the world, but accepts responsibility for everything essential that he meets."[61] This is the image of John Adams, his round face flushed, arguing passionately for the defense in a new courthouse on Queen Street in Boston, whatever the risk to his life and reputation.

Contemporary America affords its own stories of "grace under pressure" (Ernest Hemingway's definition of courage).[62] Jere Longman wrote *Among the Heroes* precisely because he wanted to publicize and preserve the courageous example of the passengers on Flight 93. "It seemed," he said, "that someone ought to write about these remarkable people. Many years from now, their brave uprising will surely be remembered as a defining moment in American history."[63] Actually, their example has already had an ameliorative effect. Ed Figura, a 55-year-old salesperson who visited the crash site a month after the flight was hijacked, acknowledged, "Just the thought of people on an airplane saying, 'We're not going to let these guys get away with this,' makes you want to live your life better than you had been."[64]

In an earlier era, Plutarch's *Lives* was a popular vehicle for instilling character.[65] Today, a nonprofit organization called the Giraffe Project circulates stories of ordinary people who stick their necks out for the common good. They include truck drivers, retirees, artists, doctors, homemakers, students, and teachers.[66]

Students may especially be affected by stories of kids like themselves overcoming challenges. Among the stories the Giraffe Project celebrates on its Web site is that of David Levitt, who, at 11 years old, decided to do something about feeding the hungry. David inquired about having his school donate all the food that was left over in the cafeteria each day. He received the same answer as several adults who had tried to get the school to donate: "Too much red tape." Unfazed, he went directly to the school board and got them to agree to donate food from the 92 schools in the county. When his accomplishment made the local papers, some classmates ridiculed him. He persisted anyway, enlisting the aid of restaurant owners and supermarkets in his efforts. Even at his bar mitzvah, he asked guests to bring food donations. More than 500 pounds of food were collected.[67]

"In stories back to the dawn of time," said Anne Medlock, founder and president of the Giraffe Project, "the healing of the wasteland has come only when someone refuses to be passive and summons up the courage to ignore all the naysayers, go forth, and slay whatever dragon has scared everybody else into terrified passivity. We need those brave blazers of trails, those people who are true heroes."[68] But can reading stories about the courage of others guarantee that we ourselves will display courage in a crisis, or does it take something more? Does it take practice?

Aristotle believed in the value of practice. "It is by habituating ourselves to make light of alarming situations and to face them," he said, "that we become brave, and it is when we have become brave that we shall be most able to face an alarming situation."[69] Many modern observers agree. Kidder and Bracy compared courage to a muscle that gets stronger with use.[70] "You gain strength, courage and confidence by every experience in which you really stop to look fear in the face," they approvingly quoted Eleanor Roosevelt. "You are able to say to yourself, 'I lived through this horror. I can take the next thing that comes along.'"[71]

Such reasoning led William Ian Miller to criticize a group of parents in his town who, armed with shovels, demolished the "child-delighting snowbanks" that plows had tossed up at a local grade school; the parents feared children would get hurt climbing on them. The school had already banned footballs from the playground because the ends are "pointed." Miller wondered whether "risk aversion this excessive" may not "kill any chance of greatness in any domain whatsoever."[72]

One doesn't expect grade schoolers to develop courage by exposing themselves to the risks of, say, skydiving or spelunking, though they should be able to play in the snow or with a football. It is college-age students who would learn the most from undertaking genuine physical risks—climbing the Shawangunks, tubing the Esopus, or hiking, as my 19-year-old son and four of his friends did, a portion of the Appalachian Trail. Douglas N. Walton, noting that self-knowledge is an important goal for young adults, argued that it can be achieved just as well through action as through reflective thought.[73] At the very least, attempting difficult and possibly dangerous tasks serves as moral counterweight to a popular culture that promotes a game-show vision of life, in which the host is always handsome and genial, the questions are never too many or too tough, and all the contestants feel entitled to go home winners.

Courage presumes a willingness to risk failure. When Lion and his companions set out to see the Wizard of Oz, it isn't with any great expectation of success. They aren't sure whether the Wizard will agree to grant their wishes or even whether he is enough of a Wiz to be capable of granting them. And once the Wizard demands that they bring him the broomstick of the Wicked Witch of the West as down payment, their chances of success seem more remote than ever. But they go on, courageously refusing to surrender to their doubts and fears. Without courage, there would be no friendship, no hope, no adventure. Without courage, the darkness would congeal and witches would reign.

NOTES

1. Noel Langley, Florence Ryerson, and Edgar Allan Woolf, *The Wizard of Oz: The Screenplay*, ed. Michael Patrick Hearn (New York: Delta, 1989), 97.

2. Harold Myerson and Ernie Harburg, *Who Put the Rainbow in The Wizard of Oz? Yip Harburg, Lyricist* (Ann Arbor: University of Michigan, 1993), 87.

3. N. J. H. Dent, "The Value of Courage," *Philosophy* 56 (1981): 574.

4. William Ian Miller, *The Mystery of Courage* (Cambridge, Mass.: Harvard University Press, 2000), 5.

5. Rushworth M. Kidder and Martha Bracy, "Moral Courage: A White Paper," www.globalethics.org (accessed October 2, 2002).

6. Miller, *Mystery*, 8–9.

7. Douglas N. Walton, *Courage: A Philosophical Investigation* (Berkeley: University of California Press, 1986), 1.

8. Kidder and Bracy, "Moral Courage."

9. Langley et al., *Wizard*, 80.

10. Miller, *Mystery*, 13.

11. Langley et al., *Wizard*, 80.

12. Amelie O. Rorty, *Mind in Action* (Boston: Beacon, 1988), 307.

13. Miller, *Mystery*, 128.

14. Walton, *Courage*, 40.

15. Dent, "Value," 575–76; Miller, *Mystery*, 59–61; Walton, *Courage*, 52.

16. Plato, *Laches*, in *The Collected Dialogues of Plato*, ed. Edith Hamilton and Huntington Cairns (Princeton, N.J.: Princeton University Press, 1961), 135, 138, 140.

17. Plato, *Laches*, 144.

18. Walter T. Schmid, *On Manly Courage: A Study of Plato's Laches* (Carbondale: Southern Illinois University Press, 1992), 42–43.

19. Paul Tillich, *The Courage to Be* (New Haven, Conn.: Yale University Press, 1952), 1.

20. Gerald F. Lindermann, *Embattled Courage: The Experience of Combat in the American Civil War* (New York: Free Press, 1987), 17.

21. Lindermann, *Embattled Courage*, 17.

22. Lindermann, *Embattled Courage*.

23. Lindermann, *Embattled Courage*, 18.

24. Kidder and Bracy, "Moral Courage."

25. Walton, *Courage*, 40.

26. Rorty, *Mind in Action*, 301.

27. Miller, *Mystery*, 254.

28. Kidder and Bracy, "Moral Courage."

29. Kidder and Bracy, "Moral Courage."

30. Miller, *Mystery*, 254.

31. Kidder and Bracy, "Moral Courage"; Miller, *Mystery*, 255.

32. Walton, *Courage*, 107.

33. The account that follows is based on chapter 6 in John F. Kennedy, *Profiles in Courage* (New York: Harper and Row, 1955), 146–71.

34. Kennedy, *Profiles*, 159.

35. Kennedy, *Profiles*, 163.

36. Kennedy, *Profiles*, 146.

37. Miller, *Mystery*, 259.

38. Kidder and Bracy, "Moral Courage."

39. Walton, *Courage*, 194.

40. The Wizard's definition of "true courage" is remarkably similar to Civil War General William Sherman's: "a perfect sensibility of the measure of danger, and the mental willingness to incur it." Quoted in Walton, *Courage*, 99.

41. L. Frank Baum, *The Wizard of Oz* (New York: Tor, 1993), 123, 128.

42. Walton, *Courage*, 24–25.

43. Jere Longman, *Among the Heroes* (New York: HarperCollins, 2002), 202–04, 218.

44. Longman, *Among the Heroes*, 253.

45. Longman, *Among the Heroes*, xi.

46. Longman, *Among the Heroes*.

47. Longman, *Among the Heroes*, 31.

48. Longman, *Among the Heroes*, 33.

49. Longman, *Among the Heroes*, 47.

50. Longman, *Among the Heroes*, 109.

51. Longman, *Among the Heroes*, 148, 152.

52. Kidder and Bracy, "Moral Courage," 11.

53. The following three-stage sequence for character education is largely derived from Appendix B of Joel J. Kupperman, *Character* (New York: Oxford University Press, 1991), 173–84.

54. Kupperman, *Character*, 176.

55. Quoteland, www.geocities.com/spanoudi/quote.html (accessed November 11, 2002).

56. Nel Noddings, *Educating Moral People* (New York: Teachers College Press, 2002), 45.

57. Kennedy, *Profiles*, 266.

58. My account of the episode is drawn from David McCullough, *John Adams* (New York: Simon and Schuster, 2001), 66–68.

59. McCullough, *John Adams*, 66.

60. McCullough, *John Adams*, 68.

61. Martin Buber, "The Education of Character," in *Between Man and Man*, trans. Ronald Gregor Smith (New York: Macmillan, 1947), 115–16.

62. Walton, *Courage*, 1.

63. Longman, *Among the Heroes*, x.

64. Longman, *Among the Heroes*, xii.

65. Kupperman, *Character*, 177.

66. Kidder and Bracy, "Moral Courage," 11.

67. Giraffe Project, www.giraffe.org (accessed November 29, 2002).

68. Giraffe Project.

69. Miller, *Mystery*, 49.

70. Kidder and Bracy, "Moral Courage," 12.

71. Kidder and Bracy, "Moral Courage," 12.

72. Miller, *Mystery*, 154.

73. Walton, *Courage*, 211.

5

HOME

"There's no place like home!" Dorothy famously declares at the end of *The Wizard of Oz*.[1] That there isn't may be a damn good thing, too, given the bleak description of Kansas in the original novel. "When Dorothy stood in the doorway and looked around," L. Frank Baum wrote,

> She could see nothing but the great gray prairie on every side. Not a tree nor a house broke the broad sweep of flat country that reached the edge of the sky in all directions. The sun had baked the plowed land into a gray mass, with little cracks running through it. Even the grass was not green, for the sun had burned the tops of the long blades until they were the same gray color to be seen everywhere. Once the house had been painted, but the sun blistered the paint and the rains washed it away, and now the house was as dull and gray as everything else.[2]

Everything else included Dorothy's guardians, Uncle Henry and Aunt Em, both of whom are described as gray-skinned and glum. "When Dorothy, who was an orphan, first came to her," Baum recounted, "Aunt Em had been so startled by the child's laughter that she would scream and press her hand upon her heart whenever Dorothy's merry voice reached her ears; and she still looked at the girl with wonder that she could find anything to laugh at."[3] Why Dorothy would ever want to return to such an awful place once she had managed to get away from it has puzzled modern critics, who often patronizingly attribute the inconsistency to a lack of conscious design in Baum's art.[4]

The movie version also suggests that Dorothy's home is something less than cozy. As the screenplay notes, "The Kansas scenes were all sepia washes."[5] This gives them a grim, gritty, dust-bowl look, in sharp contrast with the later scenes set in Oz, which were shot in blazing Technicolor. Dorothy is merely stating the obvious when, stepping through the door into the bright blues and greens of Munchkin Country, she says, "Toto, I've a feeling we're not in Kansas anymore."[6]

But the oppressive atmosphere of home stems at least as much from emotional factors as physical ones. The adults in the Kansas prologue all make Dorothy feel unimportant and underfoot. "Don't bother us now, honey," Uncle Henry says as she begins to relate Toto's latest run-in with sour-faced Miss Gulch. "This old incubator's gone bad, and we're likely to lose a lot of our chicks." When she persists in trying to tell what happened, Aunt Em becomes exasperated. "Dorothy, Dorothy—*we're busy!*" she snaps.[7]

The farmhands Zeke, Hunk, and Hickory, who will later transmogrify into Lion, Scarecrow, and Tin Man, respectively, also have no time to listen to her story or offer comfort and advice. Instead, Zeke says, "I got them hogs to get in," which indicates pretty clearly just how low her problems rank on the scale of grown-up concerns.[8]

Dorothy is an orphan in a double sense. Not only does she lack parents to love and guide her, but she also lacks a place in the scheme of things. "Now, you just help us out today," Aunt Em tells her at one point, "and find yourself a place where you won't get into any trouble."[9] But because of her difficulties on the farm and with most adults, Dorothy is left to conclude that if there is such a place, it must be "far, far away, behind the moon, beyond the rain, somewhere, over the rainbow."[10]

Adolescence is the stage of life in which young people try, often with mixed results, to forge their own identities. Dorothy can be seen as the archetypal adolescent, searching for a sense of self in a sometimes confusing and hostile world. According to the screenplay, she is "a little girl of twelve," and she is even younger, six years old, in the novel.[11] But Judy Garland was 17 when she played Dorothy, and putting her in

pigtails and gingham couldn't totally disguise that fact. The tension between her presumed age and her more grown-up appearance only en-
hances the sense of Dorothy as an adolescent groping through the
murky twilight between the end of childhood and the beginning of
adulthood.

One scene in particular seems to perfectly symbolize her plight. As
the cyclone approaches, Dorothy hurries home from her interview with
Professor Marvel, "an old carnival fakir" who will reappear in Oz as the
Wizard.[12] She goes inside the house and rushes from room to room,
wildly calling, "Auntie Em! Auntie Em! Auntie Em!" There is no answer; Aunt Em and the others are already safe in the storm cellar.
Dorothy runs outside to the cellar and tries to open the door, but it
won't budge. She stamps on it with her foot and cries, "Auntie Em! Uncle Henry!"[13] But they can't help her anymore now than they could a few
scenes earlier when Miss Gulch, armed with an order from the sheriff,
took Toto away. Dorothy must face the immense storm alone.

There is an old saying: "Home is the place where, when you knock on
the door, they have to let you in."[14] Clearly, Dorothy isn't at home on the
farm—or anywhere else. Many other adolescents feel similarly disconnected. Enlightened commentators, reacting to the government's growing emphasis on standardized testing, have argued that it is the duty of
schools to help kids achieve not high scores, but a sense of belonging.
Theodore R. Sizer and Nancy Faust Sizer, for example, contended, "Belonging is something that every adolescent should expect at school. Belonging, or the right to belong, is a moral right of adolescence. . . . [I]t
is not principled to allow an unformed young adult to be a loner, to be
out of reach."[15]

Dorothy must undergo a series of trials and adventures in Oz before
she can feel at home with herself or others.[16] That is, the discrepancy
that some critics perceive between dull, gray Kansas and Dorothy's oft-
expressed desire to return to it disappears if we understand that home
isn't only a physical place, but also a state of being.[17] In gathering together Scarecrow, Tin Man, and Lion and leading them on a quest of
self-discovery, Dorothy acquires confidence in her own abilities. As
Glinda, the Good Witch of the North, tells her near the end of the
movie, "You don't need to be helped any longer. You've always had the
power to go back to Kansas."[18] She only had to believe that she did for

the ruby slippers to work. High school should teach this same lesson of magic and hope to all adolescents. The tragedy is that, for most, it doesn't even come close.

HOME-O-PHOBIA

The popular impression is that *The Wizard of Oz* is a hymn to the glories of home and family. On closer look, though, both the novel and movie reveal some doubts about just how sweet home is. Even a conversation between Dorothy and Scarecrow that is often cited as proof of Baum's sentimental attachment to the idea of home can (and probably should) be read ironically.[19]

> "Tell me something about yourself and the country you came from," said Scarecrow. . . . So she told him all about Kansas, and how gray everything was there, and how the cyclone had carried her to this queer land of Oz. The Scarecrow listened carefully, and said,
> "I cannot understand why you should wish to leave this beautiful country and go back to the dry, gray place you call Kansas."
> "That is because you have no brains," answered the girl. "No matter how dreary and gray our homes are, we people of flesh and blood would rather live there than in any other country, be it ever so beautiful. There is no place like home."
> The Scarecrow sighed.
> "Of course I cannot understand it," he said. "If your head were stuffed with straw, like mine, you would probably all live in the beautiful places, and then Kansas would have no people at all. It is fortunate for Kansas that you have brains."[20]

That this passage is intended ironically is supported by the fact that in Baum's later Oz books, Dorothy becomes a kind of amateur explorer who, with Uncle Henry and Aunt Em, eventually rejects Kansas and relocates to Oz. Contrary to what Dorothy claims in the movie, the books suggest that if you ever go looking for your heart's desire, the place to go isn't your own backyard, but as far from there as possible. At least one critic, Joel D. Chaston, has surmised that the books' encouragement of escape from home is responsible for their controversial status with teachers and librarians.[21]

The movie, despite an ending steeped in "Home Sweet Home" and "God Bless Our Home" sentimentality, displays similar skepticism about the joys of home life.[22] Consider what happens when Dorothy seeks shelter in the farmhouse from the cyclone. Rather than providing her with protection, the house itself turns threatening. Dorothy goes to open the screen door, and it tears off and flies away. Next, the window frame blows out and hits her in the head, knocking her unconscious. The house then spins up the swirling funnel of the cyclone, as if a metaphor for the flimsiness of family bonds. Finally, the house becomes "a killing machine" by landing smack on the Wicked Witch of the East.[23]

Too often, our schools also aren't as safe as we might think or wish.[24] School shootings have practically become an annual ritual, the dark, murderous counterpart to spirit week or the junior prom. On February 2, 1996, in Moses Lake, Washington, two students and one teacher were killed when Barry Loukaitis, 14, opened fire on his algebra class. On December 1, 1997, in West Paducah, Kentucky, three students were killed and five wounded by Michael Carneal, 14, as they took part in a prayer circle at Heath High School. On May 21, 1998, in Springfield, Oregon, two students were killed and 22 others wounded in the cafeteria of Thurston High School by Kip Kinkel, 15, who had been arrested and released a day earlier for bringing a gun to school. On April 20, 1999, in Littleton, Colorado, 14 students and one teacher were killed and 23 others wounded at Columbine High School in the deadliest school shooting in U.S. history. On March 10, 2000, in Savannah, Georgia, two students were killed by Darrell Igram, 19, while leaving a dance sponsored by Beach High School. On March 5, 2001, in Santee, California, two were killed and 13 wounded by Charles Andrew Williams, 15, firing from a bathroom at Santana High School. On April 24, 2003, in Red Lion, Pennsylvania, the principal of Red Lion Area Junior School was killed by James Sheets, 14, who then turned his gun on himself.[25]

Temple University psychologist Irwin Hyman noted that the one characteristic common to all the recent school shootings is that the shooters were alienated from their school cultures.[26] Although the majority of alienated students don't act out their violent impulses, "schools that permit or promote alienation," Hyman said, "create an atmosphere in which violence is more likely."[27]

To be alienated is to lack a sense of belonging, to feel cut off from family, friends, school, or work.[28] It is a feeling that, as we have seen, Dorothy experiences at the beginning of *The Wizard of Oz*. It is also a feeling rapidly spreading among young people today, a fact reflected in their epidemic rates of depression and suicide.

An estimated one in 20 children and adolescents suffer from depression, while the suicide rate among the young has nearly tripled since 1952. Suicide is the third leading cause of death nationally among those 15 to 24 years old. A government survey found that nearly 3 million Americans ages 12 to 17 considered suicide in 2000, and that more than a third of them actually tried to kill themselves.[29] "That is mayhem," said the executive director of San Francisco Suicide Prevention. "It means there is real chaos in homes and schools everywhere."[30]

Schools are generally incapable of doing anything but adding to the chaos. "It is not possible to spend any prolonged period visiting public school classrooms," one researcher wrote, "without being appalled by the mutilation visible everywhere—mutilation of spontaneity, of joy in learning, of pleasure in creating, of sense of self."[31] Many schools are in danger of becoming, in another researcher's phrase, "academies of alienation."[32]

One reason students end up alienated is that, like Dorothy, they are often made to feel worthless and in the way. When William Glasser, founder of the Quality School Consortium, gives workshops, he interviews six junior or senior high school students in front of a large audience. He always asks them, "Where in school do you feel important?" a question that seems to the students to "come from outer space."[33] Feeling important in school is just not part of their experience or expectations; feeling small, lost, and anxious is. There is "tinder for anxiety" even in a high school's "simplest routines,"[34] from going to the bathroom, where the smokers hide out, to eating in the cafeteria, where the lines are long and slow and the tables segregated by cliques.

A recent survey asked high school students who were chronically absent what they found alienating about school. Most of them indicated that school was an unfriendly place in which teasing and gossiping prevailed and no one was willing to talk to you about your problems. The students felt they couldn't approach teachers if they had a problem, that they would be ignored or told to ignore it. Teachers were seen as sarcastic, grouchy, pushy, or burned out.[35] Dorothy is in much the same predicament as these students: surrounded by adults who won't pay attention to them or empathize with their concerns.[36] And just as Dorothy responds to adult indifference—or, in Miss Gulch's case, hostility—by running away from home, so the students have similarly responded by not going to school.

Alienation from school can take other forms than chronic absenteeism. It has also been associated with academic failure, sexual promiscuity, and substance abuse. When I was a member of the local school board, the seniors went on a class trip one spring to a theme park to celebrate their impending graduation. Some 20 students were caught drinking alcohol or using drugs on the trip. One student was so out of it that he handed a security guard at the park entrance a baggie of pot and his bong for safekeeping; he later explained that he didn't want them to fall out of his pocket while he was upside down on a ride. Other students, including the class president, had spiked bottles of soda with vodka.

It is easy to dismiss these incidents as just "kids being kids," the ill-timed result of sheer youthful exuberance. But I thought then, and still think now, that they provided a glimpse into how alienated from school even many so-called "good" students are. They don't like school, don't find it personally meaningful, and so don't consider the rules by which the school is supposed to operate worth respecting. Researchers refer to this dimension of alienation as "normlessness," which occurs when students lack any conception of school rules as an expression of shared values.[37] Rather, the students see the rules as coercive, something outside themselves to be subverted or evaded.

Given the normlessness of growing numbers of students, and the vast potential for chaos that implies, schools are obsessed with devising means for maintaining control. Even the small high school out in the hinterlands that my oldest daughter attends has a half-dozen employees dedicated to monitoring and controlling student behavior: a school resource officer (that is, a cop), a behavior intervention specialist, a social worker, a psychologist, and a substance abuse counselor. In addition, the vice principal spends the bulk of her time not supporting classroom instruction, but patrolling the halls for loiterers and the bathrooms for smokers—and, in the process, coming to occupy the role of the Wicked Witch in students' minds.

If my daughter's overwhelmingly white, 600-student, rural high school has this elaborate a control system, you can imagine what kind of controls exist at bigger, more heterogenous schools: metal detectors, walkie-talkies, surveillance cameras, drug-sniffing dogs. The irony is that these controls, though designed to keep restless, alienated students in check, are themselves a further source of alienation. How would you like to go to a school where every student is treated as a potential suspect? How would you feel if your school had the paranoid atmosphere of a police state? Probably how most students feel: victimized and oppressed.

In *The Wizard of Oz*, Dorothy must cope with authority figures who are variously uncaring (Uncle Henry and Aunt Em), sadistic (Miss Gulch/the Wicked Witch), or fraudulent (Professor Marvel/the Wizard). It isn't very different in school, where teachers are often cruel or burned out, and order is maintained by a kind of military vigilance and the threat of punishment. But if Dorothy could find her way home, so can students. Only it will require more than closing our eyes, wishing real hard, and clicking our heels together three times.

HOMEWARD

Want students to feel at home? Then don't create a school so large that it is impossible for the people there to know each other. Research shows that students who attend small schools have a greater sense of belonging than those who attend large ones. They are more likely to bond with their teachers and peers and identify with the school culture. "In fact," William R. Capp and Mary Ellen Maxwell wrote in the *American School Board Journal*, "minimizing the alienation that commonly afflicts adolescents appears to be one of the most redeeming qualities of small schools."[38]

Although there is no official definition of "small," many researchers agree that the enrollment of a secondary school shouldn't exceed 800. Today, 25 percent of U.S. high schools enroll more than 1,000 students. Columbine High School had nearly 2,000 students when it became the site of the nation's worst school shooting in 1999.[39]

Anti-social behavior is less prevalent at smaller schools because, in Capp and Maxwell's words, "there is a greater sense of knowing who's who and what they're up to."[40] Large schools breed an impersonal atmosphere that can cloak the symptoms of student alienation. The two students responsible for the Columbine massacre, Eric Harris, 18, and Dylan Klebold, 17, had plotted for a year to kill at least 500 and blow up their school, but their teachers seem never to have noticed just how dangerous they were.[41]

The larger the high school, the easier it is for students to get lost. In their classic study, *The Shopping Mall High School*, Arthur G. Powell, Eleanor Farrar, and David K. Cohen found that students at the top or bottom academically were better served than the many in the middle, who constituted what they called "the unspecial." These unspecial, or average, students were lumped together in "a great gray mass" and, as individuals, "effectively written off."[42] School is to them what Kansas is to Dorothy—a place where they are invisible, where no one cares much about them or their problems. This kind of indifference is as great a tragedy as the shootings at Columbine and other schools, and even more widespread.

My oldest son, Gabriel, was one of the unspecial. Every fall my wife and I would go to open house at the high school and ask his teachers to give him a little extra push to get him off to a good start. They would stare at us noncommittally and then do nothing to inspire or encourage him. It was as if they thought our expectations for him were too high. They would have done well to keep in mind a passage from Powell, Farrar, and Cohen's book: "A good school must be morally averse to low expectations. Inside classrooms the absence of students' skill in using their minds should never be an excuse for not trying to develop that skill, whether the subject is vocational electronics or academic algebra."[43]

It is four years since Gabe graduated, and he is still, to use a popular euphemism, "trying to find himself." He has dropped or flunked out of three community colleges, between which he has worked at various low-wage, dead-end jobs. It isn't that he lacks talent or interests; he is good with cars and animals, and he likes to draw. What he lacks is confidence, the sustaining feeling that he can do or be something special. But why wouldn't he lack it when, year in and year out, in class after class, his teachers treated him as thoroughly unspecial?

As much as Gabe's particular teachers were at fault, the system of which they were a part may have been more so. The student-teacher ratio at the local high school is about 175:1, which is the norm for schools across the country.[44] Teachers who see this many students can't possibly get to know each personally. They are lucky if they can remember which faces go with which names.

Under these circumstances, school is no more a community than a bathtub is a body of water. Community means, above all, "people working together toward some serious end," which is just what occurs when Dorothy, Scarecrow, Tin Man, and Lion join forces.[45] They accomplish their goals—at first to ask the Wizard for help and later to retrieve the broomstick of the Wicked Witch—by respecting and relying on each other and caring about the group as a whole.

This isn't generally what occurs at school. What occurs there is an adolescent version of Darwin's survival of the fittest, with students competing against each other for social and academic distinctions. There are some winners, but many more losers. Anyone who says otherwise hasn't visited a high school lately and seen the carnage in the halls—the bullying, the cliques, the boredom, the gloom.

A lot has been written since Columbine about how to improve the climate or culture of schools, and most of it focuses on the importance of making more students feel that they belong. "Our children need to know school as a place where they feel a personal connection," Capps and Maxwell suggested, "a place where someone knows their dreams and fears, a place where they are safe."[46] Psychologist Irwin Hyman called for schools in which students are "treated fairly, valued as individuals, and respected" and in which there are "very low levels of . . . sarcasm, ridicule, put-down, and other verbal assaults from staff and peers."[47] Richard L. Curwin and Allen N. Mendler, nationally recognized experts on school discipline, said, "We need to transform every school into a community that actively demonstrates, models, and advocates a commitment to humanity. . . . Educational values that relate to cooperation, safety, racism, learning, altruism, and remorse must be taught and reinforced at school."[48]

Such ideas are reminiscent of the principle that the great Russian educator Makrenko followed in his successful programs for the reform of wayward adolescents in the 1920s: "The maximum of support with the maximum of challenge."[49] Another word for this is "guidance"—a combination of love and direction, and a critical factor in the development of capable young adults.[50]

Unfortunately, school districts seldom allocate sufficient resources to meet the counseling needs of every student.[51] In my local district, the ratio of students to guidance counselors is a staggering 400:1. The decisions facing adolescents about what to be or how to become it may have grown in number and complexity over the past few decades, but counseling hasn't grown commensurately.[52]

Most students get about as much useful advice from guidance counselors as Dorothy gets from Scarecrow when she comes to a crossroads in the Yellow Brick Road. As she wonders aloud which way to go, Scarecrow, hanging on a pole, says, "That way is a very nice way," and points to the right. Then pointing to the left, he adds, "It's pleasant down that way, too." Finally, he points in both directions and says, "Of course, people do go both ways!"[53]

Living through perhaps the most tumultuous stage of life, adolescents need better direction than that. They aren't likely to get it, though, from a 10-minute meeting once a year with their high school guidance counselor. So where can they get it? Researchers have known for a long time where—from "an adult friend who will pay particular attention to the individual student."[54]

The best candidate for the job of adult friend is one of the student's teachers. Counseling, that is, can be regarded as "an integral duty of the teaching faculty rather than a task for specialized counselors."[55] My ninth-grade English teacher, Mrs. Krevoruck, made the difference for me. I can still remember my happy embarrassment when she asked me to submit a sonnet I had written for homework to the school literary magazine. It was like getting permission to become who I am.

Every student should have at least one teacher who takes "a little friendly interest" in him or her.[56] Such a thing isn't unrealistic. All it requires is that teachers assume responsibility for counseling anywhere from one to 10 students apiece, the latter being the students-to-guidance counselor ratio typical at private schools.[57] Guidance would then cease to be a special event and become more of a daily occurrence, rooted in classroom contact or an after-school activity. The teacher-counselor would help the students choose their courses, look for appropriate colleges, and explore career opportunities, as well as serve as their friend and cheerleader. Under this model, the guidance office would play a supporting role, channeling information to the teacher-counselors about course offerings, the college application process, internships, and so on. Actual counseling would occur closer to the ground, within a student-teacher relationship based on shared interests and fueled by familiarity and simple human warmth. Figure 5.1 is a diagram of what such a guidance program might look like. Notice that communication throughout the program is two-way, providing for continuous feedback.

It is possible to see Dorothy as someone who stumbles because of the absence of an adult friend to nurture and guide her. Uncle Henry and Aunt Em are too busy with the farm, and the hired hands, whether in the guise of Zeke, Hunk, and Hickory or Scarecrow, Tin Man, and Lion, need mentoring themselves. The Wizard is, by his own admission, a humbug, and Glinda, though beautiful and well meaning, is something of a ditz. Lacking proper guidance from the adults around her, Dorothy ends up as most high school students do, having "high ambitions but no clear life plans for reaching them."[58]

While stuck in the Kansas dust bowl, Dorothy dreamily sings about flying "somewhere, over the rainbow." She longs to escape to a place you can't get to by boat or train, a land that she heard of once in a lullaby.[59] But as soon as she gets there, all she can talk about is going home again.

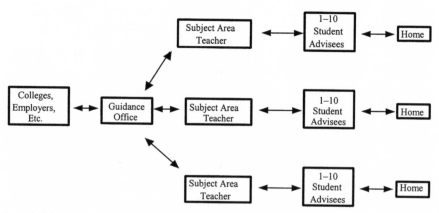

Figure 5.1   A Guidance Program Based on Teachers as Counselors

She seems to have miscalculated what independence would feel like. There weren't any adults at home willing to advise her about the obstacles she would face or the general and disorienting strangeness she would be asked to endure. She childishly thought she could just "wish upon a star" and wake up where the clouds were far behind her. She can't. No one can.

Sociologists Barbara Schneider and David Stevenson recently described many adolescents as having "misaligned ambitions." They aspire to well-paying jobs but have "limited knowledge about their chosen occupations, about the educational requirements, or about the future demand for these occupations. Without such information," Schneider and Stevenson added, "their life plans are not realistic and are often ill formed."[60] Like Dorothy when she trustingly sets off down the Yellow Brick Road, most adolescents have little idea of the challenges that await them. The result is that many never get where they say they want to go.

Parents, teachers, and other adults have a responsibility to help adolescents find their way. They can't find it on their own, at least not without a lot of trauma. Just think of everything Dorothy must suffer—wandering, captivity, betrayal—before she can reach her goal. The ordeal leaves her with a narrower, more parochial sense of home than she might otherwise have had. Undergoing one astonishing experience after another in Oz, Dorothy comes to see home as a place of refuge, a haven from, and defense against, the rest of the world. Perhaps if she had received better guidance, if the adults around her had given her the love and education she needed, she wouldn't have seen the wider world, in all its glorious strangeness, as something opposed to home, but as home itself.

NOTES

1. Noel Langley, Florence Reyerson, and Edgar Allan Woolf, *The Wizard of Oz: The Screenplay*, ed. Michael Patrick Hearn (New York: Delta, 1989), 132. The novel ends with Dorothy exclaiming "I'm so glad to be home again!"

2. L. Frank Baum, *The Wizard of Oz* (New York: Tor, 1993), 2.

3. Baum, *Wizard*.

4. See, for example, Carol Billman, "'I've Seen the Movie': Oz Revisited," *Literature and Film Quarterly* 9 (1981): 244.

5. Langley et al., *Wizard*, 52.

6. Langley et al., *Wizard*, 53.

7. Langley et al., *Wizard*, 35.

8. Langley et al., *Wizard*, 36.

9. Langley et al., *Wizard*, 39.

10. Langley et al., *Wizard*, 39.

11. Langley et al., *Wizard*, 34.

12. Langley et al., *Wizard*, 45.

13. Langley et al., *Wizard*, 48–50.

14. Susan Ohanian, *One Size Fits Few* (Portsmouth, N.H.: Heinemann, 1999), 137.

15. Theodore R. Sizer and Nancy Faust Sizer, *The Students Are Watching* (Boston: Beacon Press, 1999), 98. In the same vein, Jerome Bruner wrote, "A system of education must help those growing up in a culture find an identity within that culture. Without it, they stumble in their effort after meaning." *The Culture of Education* (Cambridge, Mass.: Harvard University Press, 1996), 42.

16. For an elegant analysis of this point, see Linda Hansen, "Experiencing the World as Home: Reflections on Dorothy's Quest in *The Wizard of Oz*," *Soundings* 67 (Winter–Spring 1984): 91–102.

17. See Witold Rybczynski, *Home: The Short History of an Idea* (New York: Viking, 1986), 62.

18. Langley et al., *Wizard*, 128.

19. It is cited for just that purpose by Billman, "'I've Seen the Movie,'" 244.

20. Baum, *Wizard*, 24–25.

21. Joel D. Chaston, "If I Ever Go Looking for My Heart's Desire: 'Home' in Baum's 'Oz' Books," *The Lion and the Unicorn* 18 (1994): 218.

22. As noted in a previous chapter, the movie's lyricist, Yip Harburg, hated the ending, calling it "tripe." Harold Myerson and Ernie Harburg, *Who Put the Rainbow in* The Wizard of Oz? *Yip Harburg, Lyricist* (Ann Arbor: University of Michigan Press, 1993), 153.

23. Chaston, "If I Ever," 212.

24. According to one estimate, somewhere between 100,000 and 200,000 guns are brought to school each day. Richard L. Curwin and Allen N. Mendler, *As Tough as Necessary* (Alexandria, Va.: Association for Supervision and Curriculum Development, 1997), 4.

25. "A Time Line of Recent Worldwide School Shootings," info please.com (accessed June 9, 2003).

26. For example, Elizabeth Catherine Bush, 14, who shot and wounded another student in the cafeteria of Bishop Neuman Junior-Senior High School in Williamsport, Pennsylvania, had endured weeks of name-calling and innuendos. See "Time Line."

27. "Alienation Syndrome," www.healthinschools.org/ejournal/ september (accessed April 7, 2003).

28. Urie Bronefenbrenner, "Alienation and the Four Worlds of Childhood," *Phi Delta Kappa* 59 (February 1986): 430.

29. Meredith Maran, *Class Dismissed* (New York: St. Martin's Press, 2000), 167.

30. Maran, *Class Dismissed.*

31. Charles E. Silberman, *Crisis in the Classroom* (New York: Random House, 1970), 10.

32. Bronefenbrenner, "Alienation," 436.

33. William Glasser, *The Quality School*, rev. ed. (New York: Harper, 1998), 49–50.

34. Sizer and Sizer, *Students*, 106.

35. The Australian researchers who conducted the survey concluded that school isn't meeting students' needs, isn't listening to students, perhaps doesn't know how to listen to them, or how to interpret what they are saying. Karin Oerlemans and Heather Jenkins, "Their Voice: Student Perceptions of the Sources of Alienation in Secondary School," *Proceedings Western Australian Institute for Educational Research Forum 1998*, http://education.curtin.edu.au/waier/forums/1998/oerlemans .html (accessed April 7, 2003).

36. Oerlemans and Jenkins, "Their Voice."

37. Oerlemans and Jenkins, "Their Voice."

38. William R. Capp and Mary Ellen Maxwell, "Where Everybody Knows Your Name," *American School Board Journal*, www.asbj.com/ 199909/0999inprint.html (accessed September 11, 2003).

39. Capp and Maxwell, "Where Everybody Knows Your Name."

40. Capp and Maxwell, "Where Everybody Knows Your Name."

41. "Time Line."

42. Arthur G. Powell, Eleanor Farrar, and David K. Cohen, *The Shopping Mall High School* (Boston: Houghton Mifflin, 1985), 173, 188.

43. Powell et al., *Shopping Mall High School*, 317,

44. Sizer and Sizer, *Students*, 51.

45. Powell et al., *Shopping Mall High School*, 3.

46. Capp and Maxwell, "Where Everybody Knows Your Name."

47. "Alienation Syndrome."

48. Curwin and Mendler, *Tough as Necessary*, 30.

49. Quoted in Bronefenbrenner, "Alienation," 432.

50. Bronefenbrenner, "Alienation," 432.

51. Barbara Schneider and David Stevenson, *The Ambitious Generation* (New Haven, Conn.: Yale University Press, 1999), 139.

52. Schneider and Stevenson, *Ambitious Generation*, 140.

53. Langley et al., *Wizard*, 65.

54. Powell et al., *Shopping Mall High School*, 220. See also Bronefenbrenner, "Alienation," 435, and Sizer and Sizer, *Students*, 110.

55. Sizer and Sizer, *Students*, 219.

56. Glasser, *Quality School*, 131.

57. Powell et al., *Shopping Mall Hall School*, 219.

58. Schneider and Stevenson, *Ambitious Generation*, 7.

59. For the complete and exact lyrics to the song, see Langley et al., *Wizard*, 39–40.

60. Schneider and Stevenson, *Ambitious Generation*, 7.

EPILOGUE
A Whiz of a Wiz

The movie may be called *The Wizard of Oz*, but the Wizard of Oz isn't its hero. If anything, the Wizard appears to be unheroic, a pathetic bumbler who can't keep his authority intact or even his hot-air balloon from floating prematurely away. Commentators have had no difficulty spotting the Wizard's flaws despite his occupying the title role. Salman Rushdie compared him to one of T. S. Eliot's "hollow men," while Lance Morrow described him as "a pretty seedy character."[1] Dorothy would seem to agree. "Oh, you're a very bad man!" she tells him after his charade collapses.[2]

But the Wizard is quick to defend himself. "Oh, no, my dear," he says, "I—I'm a very good man—I'm just a very bad wizard."[3] Although this sounds like more of his usual double-talk, there is a certain truth to it. The Wizard, for all his lying and scamming, essentially fulfills his promises to Scarecrow, Tin Man, and Lion. The curious part is how he does it, which isn't by bestowing brains on Scarecrow, a heart on Tin Man, or courage on Lion. He does it by giving them care, attention, the confidence to believe in themselves. In this, he teaches us something about teaching.

Just as Dorothy and her friends can be seen as students, the Wizard can be seen as a teacher—one, moreover, who undergoes a change in his educational philosophy in the course of the movie. He initially resembles the kind of teacher who uses coercion to try to make students learn, but he ultimately adopts the exact opposite approach.

"Coercive teachers," William Glasser, founder of the Quality School Consortium, noted, "are the rule, not the exception, in our schools."[4] The Wizard displays the harsh, autocratic behavior of a coercive teacher when Dorothy, Scarecrow, Tin Man, and Lion show up to ask his help.

It is immediately clear that the Wizard relishes his authority. He introduces himself as "great" and "powerful," godlike attributes reinforced by his appearance—a gigantic, shadowy head hovering above a huge throne on either side of which silver urns pour out flame and smoke.[5] Tin Man trembles so hard at the sight, his joints rattle.

Young students don't need over-the-top theatrical effects to be awed by their teachers. In later grades, though, authority becomes more of a struggle. A teacher who wants to cow older students may declare that his or her desk, the rough equivalent of the Wizard's throne, is off limits. Or, the teacher may emphasize on the first day of class, and regularly thereafter, that "This isn't a democracy. It's a dictatorship."

The Wizard seems almost to take sadistic pleasure in putting Dorothy and her friends in their place. Whenever they begin to speak, he bellows, "SILENCE!" or "Quiet!" or "Enough!"[6] He fits the pattern of intimidation and insult—at one point, he calls Scarecrow "You billowing bale of bovine fodder!"[7]—that teachers often follow to maintain classroom control.

But the Wizard may most resemble a coercive teacher in his eagerness to test those within his reach. He tells Dorothy and her friends that before he can grant their requests, they must prove they are worthy. "Bring me," he orders, "the broomstick of the Witch of the West!"[8]

They are incredulous. "But-b-b-b-but if we do that, we'd have to kill her to get it," Tin Man stammers. The Wizard responds by simply repeating, "Bring me the broomstick."[9] He doesn't offer a rationale. He isn't interested in the morality or social utility of the test. His only concern is that they do what they are told, however vicious or absurd.

Remind you of anything else? How about the high-stakes testing imposed by the No Child Left Behind Act? One of the chief criticisms of No Child Left Behind has been that the tests don't measure the qualities kids need to become good human beings. "Where's the test for compassion?" Susan Ohanian wondered. "For honesty? For curiosity? For moral commitment?"[10]

No matter where you turn today—politics, the media, business— these qualities are in short supply. Although schools aren't to blame for the crisis, they aren't doing much to resolve it either. Everyone from teachers to school boards are too busy trying to raise local test scores. But there are more important things in life than passing a test, such as learning to think for yourself and care for others.

The Wizard comes to realize this after Toto yanks the curtain aside and exposes his deception. He had previously conceived of power the same way the Wicked Witch had, as a means to selfish ends. Now, freed from playing the authoritarian role of "the Great and Powerful Oz," he can relate to others without bellowing. He is able to address them on the basis of their needs rather than his own.

First, he reassures Scarecrow, "Why, anybody can have a brain. That's a very mediocre commodity." Then he advises Lion, "You are under the unfortunate delusion that simply because you run away from danger, you have no courage. You're confusing courage with wisdom." Next, he tells Tin Man, "Where I come from, there are men who do nothing all day but good deeds . . . and their hearts are no bigger than yours." Finally, when Dorothy sadly observes, "I don't think there's anything in that black bag for me," he makes the "cataclysmic decision" to take her back to Kansas himself.[11]

If it is ironic that Scarecrow, Tin Man, and Lion already possess the things they seek, it is no less ironic that the Wizard isn't "a Whiz of a Wiz" until he is dethroned.[12] Forced out from behind the curtain, he becomes what he had only pretended to be. He suddenly exercises real power—the power to care and encourage and teach.

Nel Noddings, a leading expert on caregiving, said, "Learning to care and to be cared for are a major developmental task."[13] It is a task the Wizard eventually accomplishes, but that many teachers never do. This isn't because they are bad people. They are probably, to paraphrase the Wizard, very good people; they just aren't very good teachers.

We have evolved a school system that practically guarantees bad teaching. Standardized tests are overdone, and the benefits of rote learning and obedience to authority are overrated. The result is that many students hate school, or at least feel divorced from it. "They sit, largely passively," education reformer Deborah Meier pointed out, "through one after another different subject matter in no special order of relevance, directed by people they can't imagine becoming, much less would like to become."[14]

Teachers must resist the worst aspects of the system—the tyranny, the tedium, the overreliance on testing. They must try, in Ohanian's words, "to walk in the shoes of [their] students."[15] There is no educational advantage in teachers impersonating some cranky god on his throne. As the Wizard teaches us, teaching only succeeds when it wears a human face.

NOTES

1. Salman Rushdie, *The Wizard of Oz* (London: British Film Institute, 1992), 49–50; Lance Morrow, *Evil: An Investigation* (New York: Basic Books, 2003), 147.

2. Noel Langley, Florence Ryerson, and Edgar Allan Woolf, *The Wizard of Oz: The Screenplay*, ed. Michael Patrick Hearn (New York: Delta, 1989), 122.

3. Langley et al., *Wizard*, 122.

4. William Glasser, *The Quality School*, rev. ed. (New York: Harper, 1998), 8.

5. Langley et al., *Wizard*, 100.

6. Langley et al., *Wizard*, 100–01.

7. Langley et al., *Wizard*, 101.

8. Langley et al., *Wizard*, 102.

9. Langley et al., *Wizard*, 102.

10. Susan Ohanian, *One Size Fits Few* (Portsmouth, N.H.: Heinemann, 1999), 28.

11. Langley et al., *Wizard*, 123–125.

12. Langley et al., *Wizard*, 70.

13. Nel Noddings, *Educating Moral People* (New York: Teachers College Press, 2002), 25.

14. Deborah Meier, *In Schools We Trust* (Boston: Beacon Press, 2002), 12.

15. Ohanian, *One Size*, 127.

ABOUT THE AUTHOR

Howard Good (B.A., Bard College; M.A., University of Iowa; Ph.D., University of Michigan) is a professor of journalism at the State University of New York, New Paltz, and a former president of the Highland, New York, school board. A frequent contributor to the *American School Board Journal* and *Education Week*, he has written nine previous books, including *Educated Guess: A School Board Member Reflects*, *Girl Reporter*, and *Media Ethics Goes to the Movies* (with Michael Dillon). He has also edited a volume of essays, *Desperately Seeking Ethics: A Guide to Media Conduct*, and written a chapbook of poetry, *Death of the Frog Prince* (FootHills Publishing). His book-in-progress, *Guess Again: An Ex-School Board Member Reflects*, will be published by Rowman & Littlefield Education.